Poppies from Heaven...

and Other Signs from the Hereafter

Poppies from Heaven...

and Other Signs from the Hereafter

Faye Schindelka

BOOKS

Winchester, UK
Washington, USA

First published by O-Books, 2010
O Books is an imprint of John Hunt Publishing Ltd., The Bothy, Deershot Lodge, Park Lane, Ropley,
Hants, SO24 0BE, UK
office1@o-books.net
www.o-books.com

Distribution in:	South Africa
	Stephan Phillips (pty) Ltd
UK and Europe	Email: orders@stephanphillips.com
Orca Book Services Ltd	Tel: 27 21 4489839 Telefax: 27 21 4479879
Home trade orders	
tradeorders@orcabookservices.co.uk	Text copyright Faye Schindelka 2009
Tel: 01235 465521	
Fax: 01235 465555	ISBN: 978 1 84694 409 3
Export orders	
exportorders@orcabookservices.co.uk	
Tel: 01235 465516 or 01235 465517	
Fax: 01235 465555	
USA and Canada	Design: Stuart Davies
NBN	
custserv@nbnbooks.com	All rights reserved. Except for brief quotations
Tel: 1 800 462 6420 Fax: 1 800 338 4550	in critical articles or reviews, no part of this
	book may be reproduced in any manner without
Australia and New Zealand	prior written permission from the publishers.
Brumby Books	
sales@brumbybooks.com.au	The rights of Faye Schindelka as author have
Tel: 61 3 9761 5535 Fax: 61 3 9761 7095	been asserted in accordance with the
	Copyright, Designs and Patents Act 1988.
Far East (offices in Singapore, Thailand,	
Hong Kong, Taiwan)	A CIP catalogue record for this book is available
Pansing Distribution Pte Ltd	from the British Library.
kemal@pansing.com	
Tel: 65 6319 9939 Fax: 65 6462 5761	Printed by CPI Antony Rowe, Chippenham, Wiltshire

Contact Faye Schindelka at www.wisdom-of-spirit.com

O Books operates a distinctive and ethical publishing philosophy in
all areas of its business, from its global network of authors to
production and worldwide distribution.

CONTENTS

Preface

The question, "what happens after death," is one that has likely been asked by every one of us at some point in life. No doubt, we all recognize that physical life must one day come to an end. While some of us hold firm beliefs that life is eternal, others accept current lack of concrete scientific evidence in this area, as irrefutable proof that physical death means the end of consciousness. Many remain undecided, on the fence regarding the question of life after death. Most people it seems agree that a belief in an afterlife would provide immense comfort, but many are personally lacking enough evidence to fully support such a belief.

This book is written with the skeptic, the undecided as well as the believer in mind. The occurrences I've written about have more than solidified my own beliefs about life after death. In fact, the end result of my experiences following the death of my brother Murray, has been an unshakeable "knowing" that consciousness continues after the physical body dies. Despite my personal convictions, I'm well aware that for some individuals, skepticism will prevail even as they struggle to find adequate explanations for the experiences I've written about. It is my hope that this story incites conversation amongst believers and non-believers alike.

Indeed, my brother's unexpected death on the morning of November 11, 2005, has changed my life. Several minutes after saying goodbye to his lifeless body, his spirit began conversing with me. Four years later, I'm still receiving many uplifting signs and messages from my departed brother.

While I miss his physical presence dearly, the knowledge that he is spiritually closer to me now than he has ever been is a source of immense comfort and peace. Surprisingly, Murray's death has opened the door to an exciting and mysterious new world. His passing and subsequent continued presence in my life has brought with it a spiritual awakening of sorts and has added an inspirational content to my daily life that is not easily put into words. I now feel closer to the life-force that I call God. I no longer take my loved ones for granted, for Murray has so poignantly reminded me that we are all here but for a limited time. My brother's transition has helped me both to define and uphold my most urgent priorities.

The concept of writing *Poppies from Heaven* came to me several weeks after Murray's death. I had been recording the abundant signs and messages that I had been receiving from him and became increasingly convinced that my story was worth sharing. I was myself amazed at the experiences I was having and this amazement was shared by all who heard about and witnessed these occurrences. Most importantly, my deep anguish over my loss had been greatly alleviated by Murray's communications with me.

This book is more than just a therapeutic outlet for my own grief or a loving tribute to my brother. Through sharing my experience, I hope to help bring peace to anyone grieving the loss of a loved one. I also hope to help bring clarity and answers to those asking questions regarding life after death and perhaps, even provide some food for thought for skeptics and non-believers.

For those who are grieving and are open to the idea of an afterlife, I urge you to find your own avenue of communication with your deceased loved ones. It is possible.

Chapter One

Life with Murray

"Oh my god, what happened?" my brother Murray's voice sang out from the top of the stairs.

I gritted my teeth. I was hoping I would make it to the bathroom before anyone saw me, especially Murray. I raised a tentative hand to my freshly permed hair. "A good conditioner, a little hair gel, and some fluffing, and it'll be just fine." I tried to hurry past him.

He broke into giddy laughter as I came closer, then slapped his leg for comic emphasis. "Whoo-wee!" he cried. "Nice hairdo!"

"Ha,ha," I said, unamused, but I started to smile. I caught a full-on view of myself in the hallway mirror and laughed heartily.

Murray patted my frizzy curls and said, "It's pretty bad, Ragtop, but it'll grow out eventually."

The nickname stuck for the next four months, but I didn't really mind. Such was the effect Murray had on me.

Murray and I were only eleven months apart in age, so we truly experienced all of the trials and tribulations of growing up together. Our relationship wavered between "lessons in sibling warfare" and "the best of buddies." Whatever the case, we always loved, admired, and respected one another.

One particular episode of sibling warfare stands out in my mind. As teens, Murray would repeatedly infuriate me by wearing a favorite white T-shirt of mine without asking. One day I found it missing from my closet, only to find it lying in a crumpled heap on the floor of Murray's bedroom. I quickly devised a plan of retaliation.

I grabbed an over-ripe banana from the kitchen, peeled it, and threw it between the sheets of his bed. I then proceeded to roll over his top quilt until I was sure that the banana was as squished as it could possibly get. On a large piece of paper I wrote, "Welcome to Banana-

Rama," and taped it to his bedroom door. I had completely forgotten about my act of "sweet" revenge until later that night when a screeching holler declared his discovery.

Less than a week later, I was rudely awakened from a blissful slumber by the sound of uncontrolled giggling erupting from the dark depths of my bedroom. I sat up, still half asleep, when a thick, sticky liquid oozed down my head and into my eyes. The familiar aroma of maple syrup made me jump out of bed, screaming hysterically. I flipped on the light and read "Welcome to Sam's Waffle House" on a sign made out of paper towels taped to my wall. It included a crudely drawn depiction of a screaming waffle, syrup being poured over its head. The next day, I couldn't help but share a chuckle with Murray and his friend Jamie, who had acted as his accomplice. It was really quite funny that I had played the part of the 'waffle' in their twisted little scenario.

Despite his propensity for practical jokes, and his inclination for stretching the truth on a fairly regular basis, Murray was gifted with far more than his fair share of charm and charisma. This, in combination with his wonderful sense of humor, afforded him many more second chances than he probably deserved. He was more often than not quickly and completely forgiven of any perceived wrongdoing by those lucky enough to be included in his circle of friends. I'm guilty too. I couldn't stay angry at Murray for any length of time.

In my late teens I began leaning towards vegetarianism for ethical reasons. By the time I reached my early twenties, I was a fairly staunch advocate of a meat-free diet. I wanted to contribute as little as possible to the undue suffering of animals. Although a full-blown carnivore, Murray always listened openly to my arguments. He even agreed with me on many of the issues. Alternately, I made a point to remain non-judgmental of his choice to eat meat. However, despite his openness to my views, I don't think he truly understood how I was able to deprive myself of certain foods that I had previously enjoyed, merely on principle.

He arrived home one afternoon, carrying a greasy bag, full of warm, flaky bakery-fresh sausage rolls. A childhood favourite of both of ours, now painfully off limits. Much to my extreme surprise and delight, Murray informed me that these "sausage rolls" weren't made out of sausage at all, but were made with soy products and vegetables. I gasped in delight and snatched the bag from his hand. It had been a long time since I had eaten a sausage roll and these particular ones looked and smelled absolutely delicious! As I devoured several, I marveled over the fact that they tasted so "real." I asked Murray several times if he was absolutely sure that these rolls were vegetarian. He assured me emphatically that the lady who owned the bakery had told him so. I then regularly handed over money to Murray, with orders to pick up a huge bag of them. We'd munch them down together, sharing our enjoyment and our amazement that soy meat rolls could taste so incredibly delicious.

This little indulgence of ours went on at regular intervals for over two years. Then I decided to stop by the bakery myself to pick up our order. The woman at the service counter gently placed the little golden treasures into a paper bag with her tongs. An uncomfortable whisper of doubt niggled inside my gut. Tentatively, for on some level I surely did not want to know the truth, I asked her the burning question. "So, these rolls are vegetarian?"

She straightened stiffly. "These sausage rolls are made with 100% pork sausage!" I quickly established that at no time whatsoever had this bakery ever manufactured vegetarian sausage rolls. There was no way around it. I'd been duped.

Crestfallen, but not really as surprised as I probably should have been, I left the bakery empty handed. "That little bastard," I chuckled under my breath. "I'm going to kill him."

When I confronted him with my discovery, he laughed casually. "Well, you enjoyed them, didn't you?" He reasoned that as long as I didn't know, I didn't suffer any guilt; therefore he had actually done me a favor. He may have had something there. In Murray's world there was no such thing as black or white, just various shades of gray. We laughed about this culinary adventure of deceit and gullibility for years. To this day, I can't think about those sausage rolls without my mouth watering.

Being the best of buddies afforded us many a good time. We thoroughly enjoyed ganging up on Lori, our older sister by four years, who found us little more than irritants until we reached our teens. On family road trips, when we were around the ages of nine and ten, we tormented her by engaging in kicking and wrestling fights in the backseat. She'd sit squeezed into a corner we had cordoned off for her with a blanket that we'd tuck under the front seat headrest. The more she hissed at us under her breath and rolled her eyes at our antics, the more animated we'd become. She was not very fond of family holidays.

As she developed an interest in boys, our ability to get under her skin increased. We blackmailed her mercilessly. We threatened to tell mom and dad about the boys she'd invite over while babysitting us, unless she allowed us to do as we pleased. It wasn't until Murray and I entered high school and Lori started University to study psychology that the three of us really began to bond. It then became evident to Murray and I that not only did we have a wonderful older sister, but another friend and ally as well.

As young children we had our own private language, words that Murray had conjured up that he used to describe a specific look or an attitude. He painstakingly taught me his words, making sure that I fully understood the meaning of each. We'd huddle together at social gatherings, giggling over the adults present who were "nushey," "chonney," or possibly "comblesh." We were far more brave as a team, acting out in ways together that we wouldn't dare act out alone. We spent many days in devious activity simply for the purpose of eliciting wild laughter from one another.

On one such afternoon, my unsuspecting father received a "very important" business call. He was sitting at the kitchen table, telephone to his ear, speaking in his very authoritative, officious voice, reserved specifically for business dealings. My dad is a civil engineer and lives up to the stereotype flawlessly. During this particular episode of "Let's Torment Dad," a seven and eight year old Murray and I began grabbing single socks from a nearby laundry basket. As we lay on the floor, hidden around a corner, we contemplated our target. One by one, a succession of socks blanketed his head and shoulders. Miraculously maintaining a polite and business-like demeanor, Dad furiously peeled away at the socks. Much to our great amusement, he flashed seething looks in our direction, along with the odd frantic, incensed gesture for us to get lost. Of course, the more difficulty he had keeping it together, the funnier we found it, and the more relentlessly we pursued our goal. As horrible as it may sound, I can still feel the unbridled glee that engulfed us as we both laughed so hard that our stomachs hurt. Needless to say, we ran pretty fast when Dad got off the phone.

Unfortunately, I cannot report that these kinds of stunts ended with our childhood. This incessant teasing and baiting of my father was something that continued on right up until Murray's passing. I still work it a bit now that I'm on my own, but it's just not the same without my enthusiastic and ever-encouraging sidekick. I suppose it's poetic justice that I'm a proud parent of two darling little practical jokers, who I'm quite sure will put me through my own paces.

Our shared sense of humor was considered by many to be in poor taste. We illustrated this perfectly when we went to visit my dad in the hospital while he was suffering with a kidney stone. The doctors were unsure as to what was causing Dad such extreme abdominal pain. When we walked into his hospital room, he was ashen in color, lying limply on his bed, sweaty and moaning. We awkwardly drew close to his bedside, neither one of us knowing what to say. Simultaneously, our eyes were immediately drawn away from my father and up to a container suspended slightly above and behind his left shoulder. It was connected to a tube that was inserted into one of my dad's nostrils and went down his throat. The container held a vile-looking liquid that had evidently been the contents of my father's ailing stomach.

"I'll give ya ten bucks if you have a swig of that stuff," Murray said, as he elbowed me in the ribs. We quickly erupted into gut-wrenching laughter.

The attending nurse rushed in to see what all the fuss was about. She eyeballed us curiously and began to prod Dad's distended belly with her well-manicured hands. "Yup, I think the baby's coming soon!" she said, giggling.

We were laughing so hard, we had to leave the room. Poor Dad, I'm sure that had he been a little stronger, he would have thrown us all out himself.

Around the age of nine, Murray began playing the guitar. He took a few beginners lessons, and then effortlessly began playing by ear. He'd often entertain us with hilarious songs he'd write on the spot about our family, or something funny he'd recently witnessed. Whenever he was sitting idle, or while watching TV, he'd have his guitar in hand, strumming casually.

At the age of thirteen, Murray teamed up with a friend who played the drums and, much to the dismay of my parents, set up for band practice in their basement, complete with an electric guitar and amplifier. It was around this time that I began to develop an interest in singing. Too shy to sing in front of anyone, I'd stretch the microphone and its cord into the adjacent laundry room. Hidden from sight, I'd sing along to the music as Murray and his friend played. Murray was always very encouraging, so much so that he eventually persuaded me to come out of hiding.

Shortly after graduating from high school, Murray arrived home from a "jam" with friends, to surprise us all by announcing that he was going to be the lead singer for a band called *Lip Service*. When we inquired as to why he was singing instead of playing guitar, he simply shrugged his shoulders and told us "they need a lead singer, and they like my singing." Several weeks later, they loaded up an old school bus and began touring around the small towns of Alberta.

When my sister Lori and I gathered up a group of friends and drove out of town to his first gig to see for ourselves whether or not our brother could actually sing, we were pleasantly surprised. Murray seemed to have been made for the stage. He fronted the band with the confidence and style of a pro and although a little rough around the edges, his singing voice was incredibly good. There was no doubt about it. The kid had talent.

While Murray was off fulfilling his dreams as a performer, I attended College and received a diploma in Rehabilitation Services. After graduating, I had been working in a group home with mentally challenged women for two years when the singing bug bit me hard. I had confided my interest in singing professionally to Murray about a year before, and he had always been very supportive. During time off from his band, when he'd return to my parents' home for his odd week off, I'd practice my singing with him while he played his guitar.

Although there were many aspects of my job that I really enjoyed, I knew that unless I followed my dream of singing, I would never truly be happy. I answered an ad in the paper requesting a lead singer for a rock band, and after several weeks of practice I was en-route to my first gig, via a battered old school bus that very much resembled the one Murray travelled in. My parents were not impressed. If it wasn't bad enough having one of their children singing in a rock band, they now had two.

Several years and several different bands later, Murray and I decided to team up as co-singers in a six piece rock band called *Antiks*. The name was well chosen. We enjoyed several years of fun and frolic as we traveled and performed together throughout Western Canada.

To say that Murray saw the world through different eyes would be an understatement. He was immensely creative and a formidable story-teller. From childhood throughout adulthood he wove elaborate and entertaining "tales" that had his audience so captivated and laughing so hard, that in the end they really didn't care whether the tale was true or not.

One example of this occurred upon his return from the eye doctor about a year before his passing. As Murray was diagnosed with diabetes in his late twenties, it was very important for him to keep tabs on his eye health. The disease is well known to affect vision and can cause diseases of the eye, such as diabetic retinopathy. Murray came into my parents' house beaming with relief about the extremely positive results of his first eye exam in several years. "Most people with perfect eyesight have 20/20 vision," he boasted, "mine is actually better than 20/20. The doctor has never seen anything like it!" My mom and I sat riveted as he delivered his good news. "The doctor used an instrument to pull my eyeball from its socket," he explained enthusiastically. "He pulled it out about two inches. I could actually see my own face, and my other eye looking back at me!"

"There's no way that could have really happened," I told him laughing.

"I swear to God," he insisted, becoming even more animated. "He pulled it right out to here." He showed me with his fingers, a distance of about three inches from where his eyeball now sat. He elaborated further upon how strange it was to have his eyeball outside of his head, and the incredible view that this afforded him. It was a story I teased him about right up until his death. True to form, he never once backed down from his original story, in fact the distance that his eye was suctioned from its socket actually increased with each telling. It had reached the four inch mark the last time I'd heard it.

Murray possessed a flip-side though, one that carried a staggeringly pessimistic view of the world in general. Headline news stories of "the nuclear arms race" and of natural disasters affected him deeply. Very early on, he had decided that the world was definitely doomed. It seemed that it was easier for him to simply accept the inevitable horrors of this world rather than try to fight them. As a result, it often appeared as though he had one foot out the door, so to speak. This gave him the aura of someone who didn't have a care in the world, but the truth was that underneath his carefree exterior existed far more worry and fretting than one might have guessed. As is common with many very sensitive people, Murray often used his humor and casual demeanor to cover up the discomfort he felt inside.

Despite his apparently cavalier attitude and sometimes ruthless sense of humor, Murray's compassion for others ran deep. It wasn't uncommon for him to dwell for days upon some unfortunate soul, human or animal, that he had crossed paths with. It seemed that his heart was heavy from a very early age with the many injustices that pervade our world.

Chapter Two

A Premonition

Could this crappy old bus get any more drafty? You'd think that a good heater would be a priority when we're traveling in the dead of winter. There's absolutely nothing to see but miles of darkness when I look out of this frost framed window next to me. None of the other band members seem interested in talking, which isn't necessarily a bad thing. I wonder how Murray's doing with his band? It's been a couple of weeks since I last heard from him. I can't wait to talk to him. I bet he's got some more hilarious stories for me. Like the one he told last time about having all three girls he was seeing show up on the same night, or the one about the bass player they fired because he lit his hotel room on fire.

Murray's face flashed before my eyes. He was going to die. Not right away, but he would die in his prime. I was travelling to a gig as the lead singer in my first band, *Black Orchid,* when I had this premonition about my brother's death.

I can't explain how this thought became superimposed on my mind. It contained no specifics about how this would come to pass, but the essence of its content was clear: I would lose my brother earlier than I ever expected. Something was telling me to appreciate him as much as possible for the remainder of our time together.

I cannot explain exactly how or why I knew this to be true. All I can say is that every fibre of my being was confident that the message was fact. A feeling of awe overtook me as tears flooded my eyes. They weren't so much tears of sorrow, although I was indeed devastated about what had just been revealed to me. The tears were pure emotion from a feeling of being connected to the universe and despite the sad news that had been revealed to me, I knew that all was as it should be.

I've now come to realize that this feeling that came over me is indicative of a connection with spirit. I can trust the information that I am receiving, and that it is in fact coming from a higher place.

Many years prior to this, I had developed an avid interest in the subject of metaphysical phenomena and spirituality. I had begun to meditate sporadically and learned to follow the small hunches and flashes of intuition that seemed to be guiding me in my life. However, never before had I received a message with such absolute clarity. It left me completely convinced that I had just received the undisputed truth about something that would come to pass. As I began to develop my intuitive abilities, I fully trusted that I was receiving valuable spiritual insights.

I told several friends and family members about this occurrence, but I kept it from Murray. Several years later, we were traveling around together in our band, *Antiks*. While partying after a performance one night, I ingested a ridiculous amount of tequila and ended up crying hysterically. We were staying in a "band house" that week, and I was sitting in my bedroom with the door open. I told anyone who cared to stop in and listen that "Murray was going to die."

It wasn't long before Murray heard my wails emanating from down the hallway and stopped in to investigate. I spent several hours tearfully rehashing childhood memories, rambling about how dear he was to me and how I would miss him when he was gone. Murray smiled and hovered close to me, trying to offer comfort by awkwardly patting my shoulder. "Don't worry about me," he said, confidently. It was obvious that although he found this all slightly humorous, he was also moved over the fact that I was expressing such caring sentiments towards him. "So what if I die young," he told me cheerfully, "I'm having a great and full life right now!" Everyone else found my little breakdown quite humorous. Needless to say, I wasn't taken very seriously. I rarely spoke of my premonition again, although Murray and I sometimes joked about his possible early demise. It seemed that on some level, we were both aware of its basis in reality.

Several years later, while in his late twenties, Murray began losing weight from his already slender frame. The change was fairly subtle at first. His face thinned out, and his clothes became looser fitting. We were still on the road together, performing in our band, *Antiks*. He began sleeping longer into the day, and it was becoming increasingly difficult for him to participate in band practices or any other daily activities. Some days he slept right up until dinner-time. Initially we attributed this to his late-night partying and heavy beer consumption, but it soon became evident that something more serious was going on.

He'd often feel faint and dizzy and was constantly thirsty. He drove us crazy while traveling with his numerous and urgent refreshment/washroom pit-stops. His choice of drinks were generally pop, fruit juice and if it was late enough in the day, beer. One morning, while we were accommodated in a "band house" in Prince George, B.C., Murray came sauntering into the kitchen uncharacteristically early, without a shirt on. As he stood in front of the guitar player and me, peeling an orange, our mouths fell open. His bones protruded from his shoulders, arms and rib-cage. He looked like a skeleton. "Oh My God, Murray," I almost shouted, "there's something very wrong with you. You're wasting away."

"I am getting kind of skinny, aren't I?" he admitted sheepishly. "Maybe I have Aids or something," he added, as he giggled nervously.

"Well, you have to go to a doctor and find out what's going on," I told him.

"Yeah, yeah. I will," he casually replied.

He actually allowed his health to deteriorate for another few months, despite the other band members and myself insisting that he see a doctor.

He waited until we had a week off and were staying at Mom and Dad's to finally follow through and make a doctor's appointment. It's likely that my parents' loudly voiced concerns added enough weight to cause him to make the decision to go. The doctor ran a series of lab tests, and two days later Murray received a call to come back to discuss the results. He received a diagnosis of insulin dependent diabetes. The doctor informed him that he probably would not have lived through another six months with his blood sugar level reading as high as it was. Murray confessed to the family afterwards, he had been hesitant to seek medical attention for his obviously ailing body because he had been quite convinced he'd receive a fatal diagnosis such as Aids or cancer. Apparently he felt incredibly relieved that it was "only diabetes." Sixteen years later the diabetes would prove to be responsible for his early demise.

Chapter Three

Last Goodbye....Spirit at Work

"Hey everybody, we're here with the barley pops," Murray's voice sang out as he and his girlfriend, Robin, came through my parents' front door. "Not only do we have beer, but we brought our twister game too," he announced. "Robin thought the 'little duffers' would have fun playing with us." This was a term Murray often used when referring to my two children, Jax, five, and Iris, two years old. "Hey Eric, how's it going?" Murray addressed my husband. "Grab a brewskie." We all helped ourselves to a beer and gathered around the living room.

"So, how's the forty-one year old birthday boy?" I asked Murray, laughing. "Having a good day so far?"

"It's Birthday week," he shot back, "that means I get to do whatever I want for a full week." He leaned back spreading his arms wide across the back of the sofa, and smiled a devilish grin.

Robin laughed, rolling her eyes and playfully elbowed him in the ribs. "This week-long thing is new to me," she said laughing. "Leave it to Murray to milk his birthday for all it's worth."

Robin was Murray's new girlfriend. He had been renting the basement suite in her home for about six months. They had recently decided to move beyond their friendship into something more serious. It was pretty evident by the comfortable way they joked with each other that they had the friendship part down pretty good, but I detected a bit of hesitancy on both their parts regarding any kind of romantic commitment. "We're just having fun and we're going to see where it goes," was the line I heard from both of them several times that day.

Murray didn't have the most impressive track-record when it came to relationships with women, so we'd learnt to limit our expectations about the duration of his unions. I was pleased in this instance to see

15

that he had found someone who appeared to be really nice, whom he seemed to enjoy spending time with, and left it at that.

"Hey, it's Jax and Lupus," Murray called out as Jax and Iris bounded into the living room. Murray had given Iris the nickname "Lupus" due to her resemblance of a character appearing in the movie "The Bad News Bears."

She was not at all pleased about it, and told him as best as a two year old could, "I not Lupus, I Iris."

This caused Murray to laugh heartily, which only caused Iris to become angrier at him. If it wasn't for the fact that he quickly reached into his coat pocket and presented her with a little doll he had bought for her at the dollar store, she likely would have unloaded the full wrath of her fiery temper upon him.

Jax immediately threw himself upon Murray, in hopes of being treated to one of the rough and tumble wrestling matches they often engaged in. Murray responded by making a big show of diving on top of Jax and pretending to "pile drive" him with his elbows, all the while making horrific sound effects that had Jax shaking and sputtering with laughter.

"Go get Uncle Murray his birthday gift," I told Jax, when he had come up for air. He eagerly ran off to fetch it and we all watched as Murray opened his gift.

"It's a digital voice recorder to record your songs as you're writing them," I told him as he looked kind of perplexed as to what he was holding. It drove me crazy how he'd write incredible songs on his guitar and then forget them a day later. Murray hadn't been part of a band for a couple of years, which meant he'd been free to collaborate with me. We'd been working on songs for a CD of our own.

"It's perfect," he told me. "Just what I need." The satisfied smile on his face told me that I'd given him something this time that he'd actually use.

As Mom and Dad busied themselves in the kitchen preparing Murray's favorite dish of "bouillabaisse," the rest of us played numerous rounds of Twister. Jax and Iris put us to shame with their unflagging energy and flexibility. We laughed and joked as we tied ourselves into pretzels and collapsed into giggling heaps of jelly.

We enjoyed a relaxed, drawn-out family meal, complete with great food, warm conversation, and lots of laughs. After dinner, Mom arrived at the dining table, proudly displaying the birthday cake that she had specially prepared just for Murray. She had used a sugar substitute since anything with real sugar was off limits. After cutting it, she placed a piece for each of us on our plates, and retreated back to the kitchen. As Murray took his first bite, he let it drop out of his mouth and exclaimed "Oh my God!" I asked what was wrong and he started laughing. "Just try it," he managed to say. The moment that the piece of cardboard cake entered my mouth I spit it back out. It was completely lacking any sweetness or flavor whatsoever. We all burst into uncontrolled laughter. Murray held his finger up to his lips to shush us as mom made her way back into the dining room. He even tried to tell her it tasted good. Once she tasted the cake herself, she laughed along with us, and her "special" cake became the joke of the evening. She admitted that something had indeed gone profoundly wrong in her sugar substitute conversion. In spite of the inedible cake, Murray kept repeating how nice it was that Mom had made the effort. He continued trying to convince her that it really wasn't that bad.

It dawned on me then that Murray seemed somehow different. He was far more content than usual, and even seemed to have reached a new level of maturity. On most occasions when visiting with my parents, he and my dad would become embroiled in some type of argument. There wasn't a hint of one on this day. I noted that the antsy party boy of his band days and beyond had retreated and in his place sat a peaceful, mature adult. He was even drinking less beer than he usually did.

I remain somewhat puzzled over the reason for this. Certainly there was his new relationship with Robin, which I'm sure was partly responsible. Business-wise, I knew things weren't going especially well. After gaining some painting experience through working for my Husband, Eric, who owns and runs a painting company, Murray had decided to start up his own. He was presently having difficulty with back-taxes owed, as well as organizing the business in general. In the past these types of things weighed heavily on Murray and he generally reacted by being sullen and short-tempered. He presently seemed unaffected by any of it.

Murray's happiness and contentment on that day appeared to go beyond a mere response to the specifics of his life. Whatever the cause, for the first time in a long time, he seemed to be truly accepting of himself and his life in general and this made me extremely happy for him. In retrospect, I ask myself if perhaps Murray had some subconscious or inner sense that he had reached a level of completion within his life and was possibly feeling the contentment of this resolution. Consciously, it certainly seemed clear that none of us, Murray included, were aware that this particular birthday would be his last.

Four days before his death, Murray had called to invite me, Eric, and the kids over for dinner. He and Robin were anxious to entertain us for the first time as a couple. I was feeling really tired and they lived across the city from us. As I began to formulate my excuse, a voice within told me to accept. Before I could think about it, or even ask my husband for his opinion, I heard myself telling Murray that we'd love to come over for dinner. Immediately his voice brightened, with pleasant surprise. We saw each other often, but it was usually over at our house or my parents'. This time he was getting a chance to entertain us on his turf.

This was the last time I would see my brother alive. I will forever cherish the evening we shared. Murray was the perfect host, serving drinks, putting on a movie for the kids, and making his famous Caesar salad. He was relaxed and fun and full of his special brand of silly humor. Once again, I noticed that he seemed to be in a place of personal contentment. The restless energy that usually surrounded him was gone and in its place was an aura of profound peacefulness.

After dinner, Murray and Eric played a game of pool, while Robin and I sat close by, talking. The kids drew pictures for us and played with Robin's dog "Merlin," a big fat beagle, whom Murray had quickly adopted as his own.

I can still feel the warmth and love that surrounded us all as we exchanged goodbyes. My only regret is that I didn't break with convention and give him a hug. He had long before established himself as a non-touchy kind of guy, and he likely would have been embarrassed by a show of affection from me. I cannot put into words how much I'd love to be able to go back in time and embarrass the hell out of him by throwing my arms around him and squeezing him tightly one last time.

The night before his death, he had spontaneously arrived at my parents' home alone and in good spirits. He ate dinner with them and there was nothing but peaceful discourse between them all. My dad admits to also seeing a new level of maturity and contentment within Murray at that time. Robin later told me that when Murray arrived home afterwards, he was beaming over the fact that he had enjoyed himself so thoroughly, and in particular that he and Dad had gotten along so well.

We are all so incredibly grateful for these last meaningful encounters with Murray. It appears that we all perhaps had some level of awareness that he would be leaving us soon, and we were able to say goodbye before his departure. However this came to pass, these memories have been etched into our minds and hearts forever, and will be treasured by us all for the rest of our physical lives.

Chapter Four

Dead....Yet Alive?

"Mommy, I want to get dressed," Iris' insistent little voice interjected itself into my dream, rousing me from my slumber.

"Okay, okay, I'm getting up," I muttered sleepily. I checked the clock. It was 7:00 a.m. She was right on schedule. I couldn't remember when I had last experienced the luxury of sleeping in.

As I threw the covers back, Jax appeared at the foot of my bed, rubbing his eyes. "Good morning little man!" I greeted him as enthusiastically as my groggy state would allow.

"It's Remembrance Day today Mommy!" he happily informed me.

"You're right, it is." I replied. Remembrance Day fell on November 11 every year, and every year I found it depressing. Sure, I realized that the reason for such a day was to honor veterans who fought for our country. I didn't deny the importance of this, but it was still a day that I always hoped would pass quickly, as it made me feel sad.

My thoughts brightened as I remembered we had "adult only" plans to meet up with Murray and Robin for dinner that night. Being that they were both childless, and neither had to get up early for work that morning, I thought better than to phone too early. I felt anxious to confirm our plans for the evening. As the morning unfolded, I developed an oddly panicky feeling that we wouldn't make it to dinner.

"Hello?" I picked up the phone on its first ring. It was shortly after 10:00 a.m. and I hoped it would be Murray calling about our plans for the evening.

"Hi Faye, this is Stacey, Robin's friend, calling," I struggled to hear a very restrained and quiet voice on the other end. She then blurted, "There's an ambulance here at Robin's for Murray, and they're taking him to the hospital."

At first I was skeptical. Robin and her girlfriend were probably overreacting. From what I had seen previously, Robin tended to baby Murray, and leaned towards melodrama at times.

"What are his symptoms?" I asked.

"He's cold and he's white," she replied.

Low blood sugar is not uncommon for an insulin-dependent diabetic. I could picture Robin hovering over him with blankets and orange juice, Murray, slightly embarrassed, shooing her away and trying to squirm out from under the blanket.

"We'll call you when we get to the hospital," Stacey said, and then hung up so quickly I didn't have time to ask any more questions.

I put down the phone and slowly walked into the living room. The tiniest pin-prick of fear pushed its way into my awareness. I immediately felt regret for not eliciting more information out of Stacey.

"Who was it, Mommy, who was it?" Jax inquired as he danced around me.

"I think Uncle Murray is really sick," was all I could say.

Iris entered the room and her eyes grew wide. "He be okay, Mommy?"

My legs felt weak so I sat down. A feeling of dread descended upon me. "No, you guys," I told my children, my voice shaking slightly, "I think Uncle Murray may be in big trouble."

They sat on the couch staring at me wide-eyed, uncharacteristically quiet.

I quickly called my mom who had just received the same phone call. She was quite calm, under the same initial assumption as I, that Murray was having an incident of hypoglycemia.

I tentatively asked her, "You don't think that he could be dead, do you? Stacey had used the words cold and white." I felt really silly and overdramatic myself for asking the question. She assured me that diabetics often experience this type of thing, and he was likely just pale and clammy from having such low blood sugar. We both agreed that maybe this would serve as a wake-up call for Murray who needed to take better care of himself. From the time that he had been diagnosed, he had adopted his usual cavalier attitude towards his disease. While he regularly administered his insulin shots, he had long ago quit monitoring his blood sugar levels.

Five minutes later, the phone rang again and this time it was a paramedic attending to Murray. "I need to ask you a few questions about your brother's medical history," he said. Relief flooded me. Murray must be okay. I failed to consider that if the paramedic had to ask me for this information, then obviously Murray was unable to speak for himself, and was therefore not all right at all. It's amazing how self-preserving the mind can be in times of crisis, denying the facts that are simply too harsh to digest in the moment.

"How's he doing?" I asked, the optimism in my voice a sharp contrast to the seriousness of the situation.

"Well, I hate to tell you this," the paramedic began, "but I don't have a pulse on him and we've been working on him for quite awhile. We'll keep at it though while we transport him to the hospital."

I felt as though the wind had been knocked out of me. "But he's going to be okay, right?" I persisted.

"I'm sorry," he replied. "It doesn't look good."

I immediately began crying hard. Stacey's husband, Rocky, came on the phone saying how sorry he was.

"What's going on, is he like...dead?"

"I'm sorry," he said again.

I called my mom. I was sobbing uncontrollably. She grasped the gravity of the situation as soon as she heard my voice. Before I could even deliver the words "he doesn't have a pulse," she too had begun to cry. I then called Eric. "Come home now. I think Murray might be dead." I told him. He arrived home shortly thereafter and we gathered up the kids and drove to my parents' house in stony, shocked silence.

We gathered around my mom in her kitchen. "Where's your phone book?" I asked her, adrenaline coursing through my veins. I quickly looked up the phone number for the Hospital Murray had been taken to.

"Could you please give me some information on Murray Schindelka?" I asked the emergency department receptionist. "He was brought in by ambulance about a half-hour ago.

"Could you hold please?" she answered.

Another woman came on the line. "Would it be possible for you to gather up your close family members and come to the hospital?" she gently queried.

"We were hoping you could tell us something over the phone," I replied. "We were told he didn't have a pulse and we want to know if there's been any improvement in his condition."

"Well, if you were told that he didn't have a pulse, then you're aware it's pretty serious..." she said haltingly. I could tell she was struggling with how much to tell me over the phone. "I really think it would be best if you and your family could come to the hospital in person," she said with finality.

Feeling dazed, our hearts pounding, my mom and I hopped in the car and rushed off to the hospital. My dad was out shopping at the time and was therefore unaware of the drama that had been unfolding. Eric and the kids stayed back at my parents' house. Eric would have the unpleasant task of informing my dad of the morning's events when he got home.

During the drive, Mom and I allowed ourselves to gravitate towards the idea that perhaps Murray had been revived and would be fine after all. Mom was back to her original platitudes of "Boy, he'd better start taking care of himself." Denial can be convenient. It was probably the only thing that got us safely to the hospital. I drove as if on auto-pilot, somehow navigating my way precisely and decisively to an area of town and a hospital location I barely knew.

Once inside the emergency department, we were ushered into a small room. Robin was sitting with her head in her hands. "Is he gone?" I asked breathlessly.

"Yes, he's gone," she managed to sob.

My heart fluttered and the ground beneath me felt like it might give out. My hands clutched at my chest, as I fought for air. My mom and I stood momentarily paralyzed, in the middle of the room, utterly speechless. "How could Murray be dead?" I silently screamed. "I just saw him. We're going out for dinner tonight, for god's sake!"

We learned that Robin had found Murray in bed that morning, lifeless and cold. She tried to wake him up, then called an ambulance. She had also been operating under the protective cloak of denial, and had optimistically followed the ambulance to the hospital with a bag containing Murray's pajamas, toothbrush and other toiletries. Tears streaming down her cheeks, she clung to this bag like it was her lifeline.

A burning desire to see him overcame me. I frantically needed to be near him. I had to make sure that he was really dead. Perhaps this was all a mistake and he would wake up when he felt us near. Maybe he'd jump up, laughing in true Murray style, saying that it was all a big joke. For a split second I allowed myself to feel the relief that would wash over me if in fact this were true.

The attending social worker assured us that we could see him, but she seemed to move in slow motion. She spoke extremely slowly and concisely, meticulously explaining to us that Murray still had a breathing tube inserted into his mouth due to the resuscitation attempt on his body, so we were not to be alarmed by his appearance. The urgency to see my brother was mounting. I stood up abruptly, my breath coming in short gasps. I told her I just had to see him now. I felt flooded with relief when she reached for the knob on the door, and gestured for us to follow. My mom and I dutifully followed her down the hallway with out hearts pounding, our legs made of jelly.

As the social worker retreated, a nurse appeared and held back a curtain concealing a small room. Mom and I entered. My brother lay strapped to a gurney and covered by a red blanket, his mouth formed into a tiny smile by the positioning of the breathing tube. At first glance, he looked as though he could be asleep, enjoying a pleasant dream. As I drew closer, it was apparent that what lay before me was merely my brother's empty shell. Devoid of life and soul. Murray was no longer.

I kissed his already cold forehead and touched his inert body. The last time I would ever touch my brother. I sobbed out a lame and futile, "Goodbye, buddy." I had no choice other than to accept that my beloved brother and friend was gone. There has not been a time in my life when I have felt this level of complete and total despair. I had never before experienced the unexpected loss of someone with whom I had shared such a close emotional bond and I was completely overwhelmed by a feeling of powerlessness. I frantically searched my mind for some action that I could take that would reverse or erase the morning's events and bring my brother back to life. There was nothing. I felt trapped. I wanted to scream. I wanted to clobber something or someone. The tears flowed in torrents. I cried like I hadn't done since I was a child. My mom had the same reaction and to see her in this state of anguish only made mine worse.

I don't know how much time passed as my mom and I stood next to Murray's body hugging each other and weeping. Suddenly, I heard Murray's voice. Not with my ears, but inside my head. I staggered backwards a step, then steadied myself. His words immediately cut through my anguish. I stopped crying and focused on his voice.

I received a very clear picture in my mind, of Murray floating on the left-hand side of the room, near the ceiling. He was shaking his arms and legs in a goofy dance, as if to show me how free he felt. I heard him say, "I'm not in there anymore, I'm up here. Man, is it ever cool, Faye, just wait until you get to do it." His overwhelming joy was unmistakable. His humor seemed fully intact and he was evidently taking this all much more in stride than we were. The stark juxtaposition of his mood against mine seemed almost ludicrous to me, and for a moment I seriously wondered if I was losing my sanity. However never before in my life had I ever felt more lucid. I was in a state of heightened awareness, acutely present and completely at one with the moment.

He imparted to me that his death was not something that he wanted us to grieve about, because he was still alive in a way that most of us are unaware of while still in our physical bodies. He wanted me to see his transition to the other side as an adventure of sorts, where we could continue our relationship in a new and exciting way. Amazingly, despite my previous distress, I became infused with a feeling of warmth and well-being, that all was okay in spite of Murray's physical death.

Somewhat hesitantly, I informed my mom that Murray was speaking to me. She didn't have much to say about this, but it did seem to have a calming effect on her as her crying soon began to abate. It was an odd and difficult situation to reconcile within myself. There I was staring at the obviously dead body of my brother, while inside my head I could hear his voice telling me that he was still alive and that all was well. My voice of reason was also hard at work, telling me that this was just my imagination. In spite of this, I chose to rely on how the message made me feel. I felt engulfed in a warm blanket of peace and understanding, at a time where extreme sadness, confusion and despair would have otherwise been my dominant emotions. These strong, uplifting feelings were difficult to simply explain away as mere wishful thinking or the overactive workings of my imagination.

As we returned to the tiny room where Robin, Stacey and Rocky sat waiting, I remained comforted by Murray's words. I could strongly feel his presence by my side, and it was likely his energy that prompted me to surprise myself by making a very "Murray-like" joke. I gently kicked Robin's foot and quipped, "I guess this means dinner's off?" She didn't laugh, but I was able to get a tiny smile out of her. Murray was likely proud. For the remainder of our time at the hospital I managed to keep myself emotionally centered and peaceful.

Mom asked me to call Eric at their house to confirm the tragic news, and to see if Dad had made it home yet. My dad picked up the phone. "Murray died this morning." was all I could say.

He arrived by cab and appeared at the door of the small room, looking as though he might collapse. He appeared stunned, his posture deflated, shoulders sagging as he wept. My mom and I immediately stood up and put our arms around him to support him, emotionally as well as physically. The social worker appeared behind him.

I told her that Mom and I would accompany my dad as he said goodbye to Murray. Once again, we walked the short distance down the hallway, and a nurse pulled the sheet aside so we could enter the room. My dad began sobbing, which caused my mom to start crying hard again. It was extremely difficult to watch my parents immersed in grief over the loss of their son. I kept my emotions centered by reminding myself of Murray's previous words.

As we were about to leave the room, the attending nurse entered with forms in hand and inquired if we would be interested in donating any of Murray's organs. We immediately decided yes. She then asked if we were interested in donating for medical research purposes. My dad declined. Immediately I heard Murray's voice in my head saying, "Tell him yes, I want to do that. Think how cool it will be if they can learn from my old pancreas." I stood in silence for several minutes while Mom and Dad signed various papers of consent. The entire time I felt an escalating urgency coming from Murray. "Say it, say it!" he urged me. I could picture him poking me in the back with his finger. This went on relentlessly until I finally told my dad that I felt certain that Murray wanted to donate for research. Incredibly, my father didn't question me further and changed the response on the form.

Throughout my life, I've always considered myself to be quite intuitive and open to matters of a spiritual nature. Many years previous, I began using tarot cards to glean information and intuitive insight into my life and the lives of those around me. Using my intuition in tandem with the symbolic messages of the cards continues to provide fascinating and accurate readings that still amaze me. However, despite my prior metaphysical experiences, I had yet to encounter anything close to this level of clear, concise communication from spirit that I had received from Murray.

I've come to look upon this time directly following Murray's death as a spiritual "opening" of sorts. I believe that intense emotions of shock and grief can make our psyches surrender. This surrender, coupled with intense desire can cause our vibration to increase to a higher level. This increased vibration opens the door to the dimension of spirit. I believe that it was through this open door that Murray's spirit was able to connect with me.

Chapter Five

Words of Comfort and Joy

"Are you okay?" Eric whispered from across the bed. It had been two nights since Murray's death, and I'd yet to get a decent night's sleep.

"I'm okay," I said, sniffing back tears. "I just can't believe he's really gone."

"I know," he replied. "It just doesn't seem real does it?"

"I'm just going to get up for a while, so I don't keep you awake," I told him. The truth was, I needed to go have a good cry and I wanted to be alone. I tip-toed down to the living room, sat on the couch, and quietly bawled my eyes out.

The first three days following Murray's death passed for all of us in an adrenaline-induced blur. It was virtually impossible to eat or sleep. Food was the last thing on our minds. When I tried to eat for health's sake, my stomach turned into a pile of knots and the food turned to cardboard in my mouth. At night when I'd lay down, I'd be shaking so hard that relaxation and sleep were impossible. If I did manage to catch a few minutes, I'd immediately wake up with tears pouring from my eyes. It was as though the second I let my guard down, the emotions that I'd been keeping at bay all day came surging to the surface.

The other members of my family were having similar responses. My mom also had difficulty sleeping and after the third night, finally broke down and called her doctor. He wrote her out a prescription for a tranquilizer to help her relax and then finally, sleep. Mom had never been one to outwardly dramatize her emotions, but it was pretty obvious by the drawn look on her face, and the way her hands trembled, that the loss of her son was affecting her deeply. She attempted to console herself and the rest of us by focusing on the fact that Murray was now in a place where the discomforts of ill health could no longer affect him.

Murray had often confided in her about just how poorly he had felt.

My dad appeared to be diverting his grief by sifting through the mountains of paperwork that had been left behind from Murray's painting business. It appeared that as long as he had something tangible to focus upon, he could keep his mind off his loss.

The rest of us spent much time sitting in my parents' living room, sharing stories about Murray. The kids, who seemed somewhat oblivious to what was going on, continued to play amongst themselves as usual and created welcomed diversions for all of us as we prepared snacks for them and catered to their various needs. As a family we were all dealing with a level of shock and grief that was well beyond anything we had shared previously.

"We need to take an outfit to the funeral home," my Dad told us shortly after coming through the door. He had been to the funeral home to make arrangements. "They need something to dress Murray in for the viewing before the cremation."

Immediately my mom sprang into motion, searching for something appropriate to clothe Murray's body in.

"They say he needs underwear too," my Dad shouted after her as she bustled down the hall. He followed her and they disappeared into their bedroom.

They re-appeared in the living room, holding a bundle of clothing. One by one they began laying the items over the back of the couch. I gasped in horror as I took in the items they had chosen. Murray's musty, beige, graduation suit lay under a pair of pitifully wrinkled sky-blue jockey shorts, that were undoubtedly several sizes too big for Murray.

"What the hell are you guys thinking?" I asked incredulously. "Old, worn out, baggy undies for your dead son? For God's sakes, if he needs underwear, I'll run down to Zellers and grab him a new pair. Surely to God we can do better than this," I said, my voice becoming shrill. "Murray hated wearing that suit way back then. He'd be absolutely mortified to know this was the last outfit he'd ever wear!"

"Those underwear are perfectly fine," my Dad rallied back.

"They've hardly been worn. I outgrew them a long time ago".

The sheer insanity of the situation hit me and I exploded into hysterical laughter. Yes, it was very clear. We were all punch-drunk from shock and lack of sleep. My parent's were obviously no exception. Eric started laughing along with me, and we both acknowledged how good it felt to let go of some of the stress. We all agreed that Murray would likely find the situation hysterical. I felt quite sure at that moment that he was laughing right along with us. Eric offered up the suggestion of dressing Murray in something he'd been comfortable wearing in his day to day life. We settled upon the new pajamas he had received for his Birthday. He had apparently been raving about how comfy they were. We decided to forgo the underwear all together. Rather fitting I think, as Murray was known to often go "commando."

On the third sleepless night since Murray's death, I spoke with him again. I lay on my bed, utterly exhausted, finally beginning to let go. In a pre-sleep stage, I saw what appeared to be swirls of smoke appearing on the screen of my closed eyelids. This was quite different from merely imagining something. I could actually see this vision clearly unfolding like a movie, behind my closed eyes. Behind these smoky swirls, the outline of a figure began to appear. This outline was piercingly bright, made up of a vibrant orange and yellow, and only became visible as the smoky fog passed in front of it.

A surge of overpowering love and emotion enveloped my entire being, until I felt as though I could burst. Tears of joy sprang to my eyes. Murray! He was contacting me again. As before, I didn't hear him with my ears. Our entire conversation unfolded in my mind, conveyed to me through his speaking voice, as well as what felt like a telepathic transfer of thought and feeling from his mind to mine. It was accompanied by what I can only describe as an indisputable knowing that I was communicating with my brother. I got the sense that this time Murray was speaking to me from a higher or more expanded position within the afterlife dimension than the one he had been in while communicating with me at the hospital. It seemed he had progressed to a higher level of consciousness and understanding.

He told me that it had been his time to go, that each death is orchestrated in perfect timing for the soul. He didn't want me to feel sad because he wasn't. He now resided in a dimension of wonderment and joy where all negativity of a physical nature had been left behind with his earthly body. He said that while I was still residing in the physical dimension, I couldn't imagine just how it is in the afterlife, that trying to explain it to me from his new perspective was a bit like trying to describe an apple to someone who only knew oranges. The dimension he now found himself in was so very different from the physical dimension, that the physical mind was simply not capable of completely understanding it's properties. He insisted that when it's my time to cross over, I would experience its splendor myself, and would fully understand all that he was now trying to convey to me. He repeatedly impressed upon me that upon arriving on the other side, he realized that he was in the "real" place, and that his physical life on earth was now the equivalent of a dream. Again, he expressed that this is very difficult to understand from an earthly perspective. He conveyed to me a process of life review that he engaged in. No judgment other than his own was exercised during this process, and even this occurred within the context of an expansive and compassionate viewpoint. He was also able to experience his choices and actions from the perspective of each consciousness involved and thus evaluate them. According to him, the greatest transgression we can commit is a failure to love ourselves, as all other transgressions emanate from this one. If we don't love ourselves, we will commit all sorts of unkind acts towards others. When we fully love ourselves, we naturally treat others in a loving manner. He told me that while on earth, in a physical body, he didn't grasp just how powerfully creative a being he really was, but understands fully now that he is observing all from a much broader vantage point. He wanted me to understand and embrace the concept that we create all of our experiences here on earth ourselves, not just in a metaphorical sense, but in a real, tangible, physical way. He said that he was going to help guide me in making this realization and help me to put it to use in my life. He wanted me to realize that my life could be absolutely anything I wanted it to be and that through the direction of my thought, I could attain anything I could mentally conceive of.

He let me know that he'd be with me always and all I had to do was think about him and he'd be right there with me. He told me that he could feel all of the love that I held for him in my heart and finished our exchange with the exact words, "From where I am, I can see your light shining brightly." As I expressed my unending love and my gratitude for the exchange we had just shared, I felt a deep and profound connectedness with my brother and the loving source of All That Is. As a cocoon of peace and contentment surrounded me, I miraculously fell into a blissful, healing sleep for the first time since his death.

Chapter Six

Let The Signs Begin!

Another sleepless night. I swear, between not eating and not sleeping, I truly don't know whether I'm coming or going these days. Perhaps I'll just get up. Maybe Murray will meet me half way up the stairs. Ha ha, that's a good one. Then again,.. you just never know.

"Hey honey, can't sleep?" Eric mumbled through his pillow. "Everything okay?"

"Yeah, I'm just going to get up for a while," I told him. Darn, I thought to myself, I'd woken him again. It was one thing for me to go without sleep, but I certainly didn't want to keep everyone else up too. As quietly as I could, I slid out of bed.

The floor felt cold beneath my feet as I stepped off the carpeted stairs. Without thinking, I plodded straight for the dining room window. I had established a little ritual on these sleepless nights. I'd gaze out of the window into the darkness of the night, trying to process all that had transpired. A streetlight stood on the corner of our property, directly in my line of vision and over and over, I'd ask Murray to communicate with me through this light. Nothing happened, other than blurred vision and tears. This night was no exception. I headed back to bed.

It was the morning before Murray's funeral, and somehow, Eric and I were the only ones up. It seemed that the events of the past few days had exhausted everyone, including Jax and Iris. My sister Lori was staying with us, and Eric and I thought perhaps we could head out and pick up a few groceries before they even woke up.

"Wow! Just look at that amazing sky," I exclaimed as we set foot outside. "That is the most beautiful shade of pink I think I've ever seen."

"Oh yeah, that's amazing," Eric agreed. The quiet stillness of the cool morning air enveloped us, soothing our ravaged nerves. We stood in silence, our faces turned upward to the sky. "Holy cow! did you see that?" Eric's excited voice cut through the quiet. "Did you just see that streetlight go out?"

"How could I miss it," I gasped, as my eyes opened wide. "Oh, that's really amazing. This is the very streetlight I've been looking out to every night, while asking Murray to send me a sign."

"Look," Eric exclaimed again, "It's the only one on the entire street that's out, all of the rest of them are still on."

"It's Murray," I said, as I showed him my bare arm, "My hairs are standing on end. It's got to be Murray, I just know it is. I can feel him."

"Oh it's absolutely him," Eric agreed, nodding, a knowing smile on his face.

We got into the car and basked in the warm and near euphoric feeling that this incident had created for us. I felt so thankful at that moment to have a husband that was so much on the same wavelength when it came to spiritual matters. I acknowledged how wonderful it was that I could share these experiences with him with his full acceptance and understanding.

We arrived at the grocery store parking lot and grabbed a cart. We both gasped aloud as we entered the grocery store. We had narrowed the song choices for Murray's funeral service down to two songs and had been playing them both over and over trying to make a decision. Here was one of them being played for us through the grocery store speakers. The song was called 100 Years. It was by a band called *Five for Fighting.* It had been a favorite of Murray's. The timing was precise and the inherent message was received with open arms. We could both feel Murray's presence with us so strongly that we completed our grocery shopping with tears in our eyes. We remained comforted by these timely coincidences for long afterwards. Murray's use of the environment to communicate with us in physically tangible ways made my heart soar.

Several nights later, Eric and I were witness to yet another incredible and mysterious occurrence. We were in bed, with the lights on, talking. I shook my head and exclaimed, "I just can't believe that Murray is dead." Immediately after I said 'dead,' a high-pitched squeal, like a radio frequency, travelled across the room. We looked at each other wide-eyed and speechless. I ran to ask Lori if perhaps she had some kind of strange device that could have possibly made this noise. She hadn't heard the noise herself, as she had been brushing her teeth in the bathroom at the time. Had Eric not been there to witness this, I probably would have written it off as a figment of my imagination. It was so unexpected and happened so quickly. However, we both described hearing exactly the same type of sound and even agreed upon the exact point in the room in which it began and the point at which it ended.

These were the first of a series of coincidences that I have chosen to interpret as signs from Murray. Some seem to occur as a result of my asking and others just seem to happen of their own accord. Invariably they all leave me feeling lighter, happier and closer to my brother.

Chapter Seven

A Guitar Pick and an Answer

"Hey, I meant to tell you, while I was across the street in the green space with the kids this afternoon, I found a guitar pick that looked just like that orange kind Murray always used," Eric told me excitedly as he undressed for bed. "I'll go get it."

He quickly ran downstairs to where his jacket hung, and just as quickly ran back up again. "Damn, I can't find it. It's not there anymore," he told me sounding perplexed.

"Oh, no, really?" I asked him, disappointment ringing in my voice. "Maybe you just misplaced it and you'll find it later. Anyway, it's incredible that you actually found a pick. What a perfect way for Murray to say Hi."

The truth was, there wasn't anything better Murray could have used to signal his presence. Whenever he visited our home, one of the first things he'd do was grab my guitar and start aimlessly strumming. Whenever he left, we'd inevitably find a guitar pick or two left behind. He owned and cherished an acoustic twelve-string guitar that he serenaded himself with for several hours, along with a cold beer or two, before heading off to bed most nights. We went to sleep in agreement that it was Murray who had sent Eric that guitar pick.

The next morning, I kissed Eric goodbye and watched him lope down the front walk towards his truck. Minutes later, he came barging back into the house.

"The pick," he gasped breathlessly, as he held up an orange "Dunlop" pick. "I found it right underneath the door of my truck. It must have fallen out of my pocket yesterday."

"That's amazing," I said, wide-eyed, as I snatched the pick from his hand. "This looks exactly like one of Murray's favorite picks that he always carried in his jeans pocket. Do you think he could have dropped it out there one time when he was visiting?"

"Well, I guess we'll never know for sure," Eric told me. "But however it got out there, it sure is a cool coincidence that I just happened to find it.......twice!"

I could not deny it. This guitar pick seemed destined one way or another to make its way into our hands. I was quick to put it away in my jewelry box where it wouldn't be lost again.

Later in the week I received another type of message, delivered in the form of a synchronistic conversation. This message seemed to occur as a direct result of my request. As I was walking Jax to kindergarten, I became lost in my thoughts about Murray's death. He had finally reached a point in life where for the first time, he seemed to be in full acceptance of himself. He had seemed more at peace than I had ever known him to be and then his life was cut short. I struggled to see the reason in this. With a heavy heart I walked silently asking over and over, "Why did you have to die now?"

I sighed heavily, as I spotted one of the other parents waiting for us to catch up. Normally, I would have been happy to talk with him, but my eyes were red and swollen from crying and I just didn't feel like socializing. I resigned myself to keep the conversation brief. When I dew up beside him, he commented that I looked really tired. Reluctantly, I explained that my brother had just died and I was having difficulty sleeping. I told him that the cause of death was suspected to be diabetes related.

He immediately began to tell me that his father-in-law, who was in his late sixties, was also an insulin-dependant diabetic and had been for many years. He was currently in the hospital, undergoing the seventh operation on his legs to restore nerve damage from uncontrolled blood glucose levels. He went into great and gory detail about this operation, describing how the legs were cut open from knee to upper thigh, and how painful the ensuing recovery would be. Like Murray, this man had been lax in following the various routines and rituals generally prescribed for those afflicted with diabetes. As a result, he had experi-enced a myriad of disabling complications, such as problems with his kidneys, eyes, and nerve damage, which had plagued him throughout the years. As my messenger railed on about his father-in-law's many years of suffering, it dawned on me that perhaps my question had been answered.

As a family, we were all well aware that Murray's health had been slowly deteriorating. My mom in particular had constantly voiced her worry and concern over Murray's health, likely because she was the one Murray confided most of his health ailments to. It was actually baffling that in light of his neglectful practices, and prolific beer drinking, Murray hadn't suffered from obvious and debilitating diabetes related complications. Prior to his death, he had once again been losing weight and regularly mentioned pains and numbness in his hands and feet, frequent lightheadedness, and headaches. These ailments were likely signs of impending and serious health problems. Murray would have been absolutely miserable, and downright uncooperative in the event of a serious down-turn in his health. Was it possible that through this man's story, Murray was giving me a message? Could he have been trying to tell me that in passing from his diseased body while still relatively healthy and happy, he had experienced the "blessing" of leaving on a high note? I chose to interpret it as such. This would have been completely in keeping with Murray's personality. I walked away from this conversation full of gratitude that Murray had been spared any suffering and indignity had he lived longer. He was now in a place where he could not be touched by earthly sorrow, pain, or suffering of any kind.

If I had had it my way, this conversation never would have taken place. This was a good lesson for me. Often the universe has a higher plan and wonderful things can come from simply flowing with the moment.

Chapter Eight

Flowers and Butterflies

After Murray's funeral service, I spoke at length with a dear friend who had recently experienced her own loss of a close family member. She had asked the deceased for specific signs that would mysteriously manifest, leaving no doubt whatsoever in her mind that her loved one was still near. As I was sitting on my couch several days afterwards, I remembered her words. "Don't be afraid to ask for something really specific," she assured me. "They can do it."

I began to ponder what I should ask for as a sign. I felt confident that whatever I chose would appear, so I wanted something pleasing. However, I was also somewhat impatient. I wanted "the sign" to appear to me that very day. "Murray," I began. "If you're here with me and can hear this, then I want you to send me a pink flower."

I went about the rest of my day in high expectation, telling no one of my secret request. I visited the hair salon and went out for dinner with Eric. Every half hour or so I'd silently remind Murray that I expected to see a pink flower. Eric and I departed the restaurant in separate vehicles, and I continued my mantra of "pink flower, pink flower" all the way home.

I arrived home and took off my boots. My watch read almost nine p.m. I regretfully had to concede that perhaps I would not be receiving my sign today. Although I felt a little bit disappointed, I still believed that I would receive my flower at a later date. "Okay Murray," I said out loud. "Maybe not today, but I'm still holding you to it."

As I closed the closet doors, I heard Eric come in through the back door. He appeared around the corner, hand outstretched, holding a bouquet of three Gerbera daisies. White, yellow, and in the middle was a great big, beautiful pink one! I took the precious flowers from my husband and explained my earlier request to Murray. Eric wiped my tears and told me that he had bought the flowers earlier in the day, purely on a whim. My husband doesn't make a habit of buying me flowers, aside from special occasions. He had even forgotten them in his truck, otherwise I would have received them at dinner. He had also chosen the three individual flowers himself, something he had never done before. I was thankful that on that particular winter's day, the weather had been relatively mild. The flowers stayed fresh and beautiful, none worse for wear for having been left in his truck for hours. I placed my flowers in a small vase and was not at all surprised that the pink daisy survived the other two by well over a week.

Several days after receiving my flower sign, I woke up to an arctic landscape. A blanket of fresh snow had covered the ground and fine dust-like flakes were swirling down from the sky. I felt particularly sad on this morning, partly due to the drab, sunless sky, but mostly I was just really missing Murray and feeling the need for some kind of communication from him. The memory of the pink flower still fresh in my mind, I quickly decided that today I'd ask Murray to provide me with another sign. A white butterfly appeared in my mind. "Okay Murray, send me a white butterfly today." I laughed out loud. "Fat chance."

Less than two hours later I reached into my mailbox and pulled out several pieces of mail. I came upon an envelope from a long-time client of mine who I had recently read tarot cards for. She always sent me payment by mail, enclosed in beautifully decorated cards with matching envelopes. This particular one was decorated on both sides with ethereal, water-colored butterflies. Yellow, blue, and white butterflies were flying through heavenly pastel skies.

I stood transfixed. Tears of joy blurred my vision as I held the envelope to my chest. I thanked Murray once again, immersing myself in the wonderful feeling of connection to him. I could feel his presence beside me in that moment. He was always close by and all I had to do was think of him. It certainly seemed to me that Murray was privy to my most innermost thoughts and was paying rapt attention.

As I shared these signs with those around me, they were amazed and comforted. I consider myself extremely lucky to be surrounded by family and friends who are so very open when it comes to this subject. Even my dad with his hyper-analytical mind always listens intently as I relay these occurrences. Although he generally offers up little more in the way of feedback than a raised eyebrow, it's evident by his rapt attention to these stories, that he's also comforted by them.

It was my dad who surprised us all on the day of Murray's funeral when he came through the back door of his kitchen carrying a tiny fresh pansy flower. "Look what I found peeking out of the snow," he told us, his voice catching in his throat. "Who would think a pansy would be capable of growing in this cold?" he asked Eric, Lori, Robin and I as he held the pansy with reverence in the air for all of us to see, his eyes shining with tears. Although he didn't come right out and call it a sign from Murray, we all knew that it was implied.

Of course we were all quick to let my dad know. "It's a sign from Murray. He's letting you know he's still alive." Dad didn't argue as he placed the pansy in a tiny glass of water. I overheard him that day relaying the story of the pansy to many friends and family members.

The following year, the very same pansy plant bloomed again mid-winter, bearing several tiny perfect pansies for my dad.

Chapter Nine

Visions of Cookie Jars

I began to ponder the process involved in receiving signs. At times, it was simply a case of cause and effect. I would ask for a particular sign and then receive it. Other times, Murray would send me telepathic messages where he would show me a sign in my mind and then I'd receive it.

While lying on my bed meditating one night with the intent of connecting with Murray, I received a picture of a cookie jar. This would be the next sign that I would receive from him. "A cookie jar?" I asked aloud.

Murray answered, "No, not a cookie jar exactly, but it looks like one."

"This is really getting strange," I said to myself. However, strange or not, I vowed to spend the following days on the look-out for anything that remotely resembled a ceramic container with a lid of some sort. Nothing in particular stood out, but I resigned myself to keep looking.

Two days later, I was watching TV and a commercial for gingerbread cookies appeared. A feeling of knowing came over me that Murray would be sending me a sign involving a gingerbread man. It was nearing Christmas time so gingerbread men images were in abundance. I knew I shouldn't have too much trouble spotting this one, but I questioned how I would recognize it as my sign. I tucked it all into the back of my mind with the thought that I was pre-warned should a gingerbread man jump out at me.

Three days later, I arrived at my parents' house for a visit. "I won the booby prize last night at banko!" my mom happily informed me as I removed my shoes at the front door. Banko is a dice game that she plays with a group of women once a month, where they win prizes of various sorts. "I was tied for last place with another player, and we drew numbers to see who would get the prize," she elaborated enthusiastically.

"Wow, I guess you had lady luck on your side last night," I joked with her. "What did you win?"

"It's really cute," she informed me as she disappeared around the corner to retrieve it, "But I really don't have anywhere to put it. It's yours if you want it."

As she appeared in front of me, holding her prize, I almost fell over. In her hands she held a ceramic cookie jar with ten gingerbread men on the lid. When I lifted the lid, I saw that it wasn't a cookie jar after all, but a huge gingerbread-scented candle, therefore it only "looked like a cookie jar."

My legs felt weak beneath me and I sat down. "You won't believe this mom," I told her as I tried to catch my breath, "But I think Murray somehow knew you'd win this thing and would pass it on to me. He told me he'd be sending me a cookie jar and then a gingerbread man. I didn't know they'd be part of the same sign. This is just too perfect. There's just no denying that he's still with us."

"That is unbelievable," my mom replied as she too grabbed as seat. "Boy, he's sure been busy it seems." She shook her head in disbelief. "You know all of these signs are really helping me to believe he's still here. I can't tell you how much it helps knowing this. She then added, "I talk to him too you know, and there are times where I think I hear his voice talking back to me."

"He's alive and well in spirit mom. He can hear everything you say to him, and when you think it's him talking to you, it is," I told her. "The more you trust this, the more contact you'll have."

We marveled over the fact that those in the afterlife would be interested in such seemingly trivial and inconsequential aspects of our lives. We laughed to think that while Murray was reveling in the awesome expansiveness of the hereafter, he still somehow found time to keep track of Mom's banko games. Possibly his intended message was just that. Nothing is too trivial or inconsequential. He is present in our lives always and anytime.

Mom and I shared this uplifting occurrence with the rest of the family and they were all as impressed as we were. Even my dad had to admit that it was pretty uncanny how mom won the cookie jar/candle right on the heels of my messages from Murray.

We all agreed that the candle would make a perfect centerpiece for our first Christmas Eve without Murray. There was no denying it was a difficult night. We focused on the kids, and the fun they had opening gifts and frolicking around the Christmas tree. Robin, Stacey and Rocky dropped in and we exchanged gifts as well as updates about how we were all managing without Murray. The gingerbread candle on the table served as a poignant reminder that although we couldn't physically see him or hear him making his special jokes, he was still aware of our lives, right down to the finest detail. We were quite sure he was celebrating along with us on that night.

Chapter Ten

Red Salmon

As I idly sorted through the contents of the box of mementos on my parent's dining room table, I suddenly stopped short, and gasped. "Oh my god, mom, how come I've never seen this picture?" I called out. "I didn't know there were photos taken of Murray at Fairmont."

I held up a photo of my brother. It had been taken about two weeks prior to his death, while he and Robin had accompanied my parents on their yearly trip to their timeshare in Fairmont, British Columbia.

"You mean you didn't see that?" my mom asked incredulously.

"No," I told her. "And I can't tell you how thrilled I am to find a recent picture of him."

"He sure looked sick, didn't he?" my mom said shaking her head sadly.

"Yeah, did he ever," was all I could say. I honestly hadn't realized back then just how run down he had been.

"It was taken the day Dad took us to see the dying Salmon," mom informed me. The photo showed a rather bedraggled, unhealthy-looking Murray, standing next to a creek rife with bright red Kokanee. These Land Locked Salmon return to their place of birth to spawn and then die. The spiritual symbolism of this photograph absolutely screamed out to me, and I found myself moved to tears.

My parents had owned the timeshare for about fifteen years. Lori and I had joined them on several occasions, but this was the first time for Murray. Their time slot was booked the same time every year, late October, and therefore at my father's insistence, the dying salmon were always on the list of things to go and see while in Fairmont.

My parents had invited my family as well, but this time I declined. It was important for Murray and Robin to go alone so that they could experience the luxury of their own suite. Mom tried to convince me but I was insistent that it was Murray's turn to go. Once again, I seemed to know that Murray's time was limited, or at the very least that time was of the essence. After his passing, we were glad that Murray was able to experience this holiday before he left this world.

Two weeks after I found the photo of Murray, I sat on Jax's bed with his first library book in my lap. It was called "Salmon Creek." He had come home from kindergarten that day and proudly announced that for the first time, he had signed out a book all by himself. When we sat down to read it, I couldn't believe my eyes. The cover looked astonishingly similar to the creek filled with the red salmon in Murray's photo. If I could have sketched in Murray's figure standing on the riverbank, I would have had a near mirror image. I tried valiantly to hold back my tears while reading it to my son, but much to his displeasure, I failed pitifully.

"Mommy," he said. "Can you stop crying please, I can't understand the words."

"I'm sorry sweety," I told him through my tears. "This book is reminding me of Uncle Murray." The story was a poetic tale about the salmon's journey to return to the very place of their origin in order to complete their life cycle and die.

After I pulled myself together and made it through the story to satisfy Jax, I went and sat alone with the book. "What are the chances, that on his very first library pick ever, Jax would pick this specific book?" I asked myself. When I queried Jax about why he had felt compelled to choose this particular book, he said, "It was closest to me, Mom." I was left to conclude that my son isn't terribly particular about the books he reads, and spirit certainly works in mysterious ways.

I often wonder if Murray had any inkling that his own life cycle was soon coming to a close when he gazed upon the dying salmon at Fairmont. When I look at this photograph of him, I can't help but think that he likely felt much like the red fish; physically exhausted, worn out, and ready to surrender at the end of an arduous journey.

Several days after finding this photo, I called Robin to ask her if she wanted a copy.

"I already have one that was taken on my camera," she told me. "He sure looks unhealthy doesn't he?" she commented. "You know, when we were there, I could tell he wasn't feeling good, but he kept it to himself. I didn't hear him complain once. Man, he was such a great guy."

Our conversation turned to the kids and I inquired as to how her dog, Merlin, was doing. Then an uncomfortable silence followed.

"I have some news to share," she told me hesitantly. "I feel kind of strange telling you about it though."

"You can tell me," I encouraged her.

"I'm seeing someone. His name is Jason, and he makes me really happy. He reminds me a lot of Murray," she blurted out.

"That's great Robin," I told her enthusiastically. I assured her that we fully expected her to move on with her life and that we also knew that Murray would want nothing more from her than her happiness.

She spent the remainder of the conversation filling me in about the details of her new relationship. Apparently their first date had been on Christmas Eve, after she had left our house. Again, she had been hesitant to tell us about it that night as it made her feel uncomfortable.

"You have to know," I told her, " Murray's giving you his full blessing to move on and have a wonderful life, and who knows... maybe even has his hand in this."

As time passes, we continue to keep in touch with Robin and we've been extremely pleased to see that her relationship with Jason continues to thrive.

Chapter Eleven

Musical Signs

A few days after Murray's passing, Eric, Lori, the kids, and I buckled ourselves into the car for the short drive over to my parents' house.

"So Eric," I asked my husband. "You're going to go with Lori and Dad to view Murray's body at the funeral home at noon?"

"Yeah, I'd like to, that is if it's okay with everybody," he replied

"Absolutely," Lori interjected. "Faye, you're not coming?" she asked me.

"No," I told her, shaking my head sadly. "I said goodbye to him at the hospital, I honestly don't think I could bear to see his lifeless body again. Besides, I want to stay with mom and help out with kids, she's looking pretty worn out, and they might be a bit much for her today."

We had just turned onto the main road leading from our home, when I leaned in closer to the car speaker, and reached for the radio's volume knob. "Lori! Listen to the song that's playing!" I nearly shouted into the back seat, where Lori sat squeezed in next to the kids.

"It's *The Chipmunk Song* she exclaimed in awe. You and Murray used to play this song over and over again when you were little."

"Remember the record sleeve with the Happy Crickets on the front? Murray and I would take turns holding it when we listened to this song. You know, I think we still have that record downstairs at Mom and Dad's somewhere."

"It's pretty amazing that on this short trip over to your parents' house, you guys are actually hearing this, don't you think?" Eric inquired.

It was amazing. And what made it even more so was that it was being played on an adult pop/rock radio station. *The Chipmunk song* was never played on any radio station; in fact it had been many years since we had heard this song at all. I cannot think of a better way for Murray to let us know that he was with us on that difficult day.

A little over a month later, I received another musical sign from Murray. Eric and I had taken the kids skating at the outdoor rink at our neighbourhood's community centre. It was an especially beautifully winter's day and as I laced up my skates, my thoughts drifted to Murray. He had accompanied us the previous year on our last skating excursion of the season, entertaining us all with his hilarious parody of an ice dancer. He had been an accomplished skater from years of playing hockey, and was therefore quite convincing in his role. He had left me in stitches, tears in my eyes, doubled over at the edge of the ice.

Murray was the only thing on my mind as I approached the rink. My foot had just hit the ice, when one song ended and another began to play over the outdoor speakers surrounding the skating rink. I almost lost my balance. I could hardly believe what I was hearing. Platinum Blonde's *Standing in the Dark* began blaring from the speakers. This was the first cover song that I remember seeing Murray perform in his first rock band. He had a special affinity for it, due to his possession of the necessary range and the tonal qualities of his voice. Early in his career, he bore a strong resemblance to the lead singer of Platinum Blonde. Murray wore his blonde hair puffed up on top, as the back and sides cascaded past his shoulders. His stage attire consisted of cropped jackets and skin tight brightly colored pants that he wore tucked into pointy-toed boots. Even while Murray was alive, this song always evoked within me a strong association with him. I felt my mind drift back to the eighties. Murray was certainly right in his element. He milked his situation for everything it was worth, traveling from city to city, staying in hotels, performing and partying every night with flocks of spiky-haired, spandex clad women. Life as far as he was concerned, just didn't get any better.

I smiled in thanks for the hello from Murray, and brushed away my tears. I enjoyed my skating experience all the more knowing that Murray was with us. I couldn't get the vivid picture out of my mind of him making goofy, over exaggerated attempts at graceful movement with his hands, as he comically performed fancy intricate dance steps.

I returned home, still aglow from hearing the song and pleasantly tired out from the fresh air and exercise. I turned on the TV for the kids, leaving it on the immediate channel. A movie came on about a girl grieving the loss of her brother after his sudden death. "Unbelievable," I muttered under my breath as I stood transfixed, staring at the TV. I smiled at the incredible timing involved. Combined with my previous sign, this was a synchronistic event that strongly reaffirmed Murray's presence with us that day.

Shortly after Murray's death, I heard for the first time a song by the band Lifehouse called *You and Me.* It instantly reminded me of Murray. The chord progression, lyrics and the strumming pattern of the guitar sounded so much like songs Murray had written in the past. The singers voice was also similar in timbre to Murray's. I often hear this song playing the instant that Murray's name comes up or when I'm in need of some comfort or assurance from him.

On one such occasion, I was driving in traffic when an ambulance pulled in front of me. I teared up, reminded of Murray's last ride in an ambulance. As though in direct answer to my pain, *You and Me* began to play on the radio, filling me with a sense of awe, and the feeling that Murray was near. Later that day, while sharing lunch and animated conversation with my friend Marni, I began to tell her about this song that kept popping up at the most opportune of times. Before I could tell her the name of it, she stopped me, her eyes filled with tears. "Don't tell me, I know what it is. There's a song that I just learned to play on guitar. It's actually the first song that I've ever played all the way through, and I've felt Murray's presence whenever I'm playing it." There was a palpable charge in the air as she paused slightly before revealing what I already suspected. It was the same song. We both felt the unmistakable tingly, euphoric feeling that let us know that Murray was close by. We spent the remainder of our lunch united in our awe over the mysterious ways of spirit.

This song is one of several that serves as a powerful sign that Murray is present, many months now after his passing. The other day, as I pulled up in front of my house, I had an overwhelming impulse to switch to an alternate radio station, just as I was about to turn the car off. I absolutely knew that I'd receive a sign from my brother. I jabbed the button that would instantly connect me with another station. Sure enough, *You and Me* was playing.

Murray was a gifted singer/songwriter, so I shouldn't have been surprised to receive musical signs from him. I've also compared stories with others who have lost loved ones, and I've found that those on the other side often seem to use music as a means of communication. Perhaps this is because of the specific vibration of music itself, which somehow helps to facilitate the communion between this side and the other.

Chapter Twelve

Through a Child's Eyes

Witnessing my two children deal with the loss of their only uncle has been a unique and enlightening experience. Jax watched with an open and honest curiosity as all of the adults around him attempted to deal with the death of his Uncle Murray. "Why are you crying mommy?" he asked on more than one occasion. "How come you're not hungry?" he wanted to know when Grandma didn't feel like eating. He was party to all of our conversations as we gathered together and tried to make sense of the tragedy that had transpired. He tried his best to alleviate our pain, and some of his awkward attempts did succeed at times.

It was the morning of the funeral, and he was sitting on my bed watching me as I tried to get dressed. "Mommy how come you keep changing your clothes?" he asked.

"I can't make up my mind, Jax. Nothing I put on looks or feels right," I told him as I held back tears.

"Wear that," he told me as I slipped a dark green turtleneck over my head that matched a lighter green skirt I had put on.

"You're sure sweetie? Mommy looks okay?"

"You look real pretty," he assured me.

"Okay, this is it then," I told him as I surveyed myself in the mirror.

In truth, I really didn't care all that much what I wore, as long as I looked presentable enough to pass. "What exactly is one supposed to wear when saying goodbye for the last time to their brother?" I wondered aloud.

"Mommy, I know how you can not feel sad anymore," Jax's voice drifted across the room. "Just pretend that it was somebody else who died and not Uncle Murray."

It took everything within me not to burst out in laughter. "Yes Jax,"

I told him. If I could pull that off, it would help." It felt good to smile.

He also surprised us with a statement that almost seemed heartless had it not been so unabashedly honest. As we sat at my parents' house after the funeral, Lori and I openly weeping, Jax responded proudly with, "Isn't it weird that I'm not even feeling sad about Uncle Murray dying?" At his young age, Jax hadn't experienced anything this traumatic. He would come to miss Murray's presence soon enough.

Jax often talks about death and the afterlife, so there is no doubt that Murray's passing has affected him. He tells me that he knows Murray can still see and hear us and that he is in a place that looks like a "park." He also has told me that he remembers being in this same place before he came down to be my baby. As a child, he seems to deal more with the facts of Murray's death; the emotional content has been somewhat suspended. Just recently he has actually started to make comments about missing Murray. When he sees or hears something funny, he often says Uncle Murray would have liked that, or that Uncle Murray would do that, etc.

Recently he told me upon waking that Uncle Murray had come into his room the previous night right before he drifted off to sleep. He adamantly insisted that he wasn't dreaming as he calmly recited his account of this encounter. He says Murray was wearing his backwards baseball cap, and although he wore clothing, Murray's form was transparent. "He had a beer in his hand mom," he added seriously. He apparently focused upon Murray for a couple of seconds, and then his form vanished. I continue to be struck with just how nonplussed Jax appears to be by this experience. When I asked him why he thought Murray appeared to him that night, he simply shrugged his shoulders, casually saying, "I have no idea."

Iris was only two and a half at the time of her uncle's death. At his funeral service, she pretended to read aloud from a book that had been given to her by a thoughtful cousin of mine prior to the service. She made an effort to mimic my uncle who was giving the eulogy. As she observed those around her crying and wiping away their tears with a tissue, she did the same, delicately dabbing at her own eyes. While she was able to verbalize the fact that her uncle had died, she was certainly at a loss to fully understand this.

She is always intent upon buoying me up with encouraging words whenever she sees me feeling sad about Murray's death. On the day I'd received the autopsy report in the mail and was sitting at the table crying, she looked up at me and said, "Mommy, don't be sad, Uncle Murray is right here." She pointed next to her chair and added, "Oh boy, look how tall he is." She tilted her little blonde head way back to look towards the ceiling.

One morning while eating her breakfast, she turned around to gaze at a photo of Murray that was sitting on a table directly behind her. She began to giggle as she told me that Murray was tickling her back. She said, "I think he likes me, Mommy."

"Oh yes," I assured her. "He certainly does."

When Iris tells me that Murray is near, there is such earnestness in her voice that I can't help but believe that she is really seeing him. One night Eric and I had been up countless times with her as she was sick with a cold and had a cough that would not abate. It was around four a.m. when I tucked her in for what I hoped would be the last time. I watched her as she appeared to settle in and relax into a sleepy state. I returned to bed and was just starting to drift off myself, when I heard the sound of joyful laughter coming from her room. I clearly heard her say, "Look Mommy, Uncle Murray is in my window. He says that he's watching over our house. Isn't that sweet?" I didn't get out of bed to check on the situation due to extreme fatigue, but in light of the blissful silence that followed, I assumed that she was fast asleep and dreaming. When I asked her about it the next morning, she didn't remember anything. I believe that Murray is "watching over our house" and appeared to Iris that night in her dream state to tell her so.

I've explained to Jax and Iris my beliefs about the afterlife, yet I've also told them that they should decide for themselves what to believe about spiritual matters. They seem to be more than willing to accept that

Murray is residing in Heaven, and that his spirit is always around, watching over us. They often remind me that Murray is still with us, whenever I'm feeling low and missing him.

Chapter Thirteen

Magical Mail Delivery

We all accepted that Murray's death was diabetes related, but I hated to think that his trademark cavalier attitude contributed as well. He certainly drank far too much beer for someone with his health issues, and it was anyone's guess just how long it had been since he had last seen a doctor for a checkup. His blood glucose monitor had not been equipped with working batteries for at least a year or more. I knew this because we had made a goofy game of sorts out of testing all of our blood glucose levels at family gatherings.

"Hey Murr, grab your glucose meter, we're gonna test our blood sugars," I usually called out at some point during one of our dinner parties at Mom and Dad's. "Lets check our levels."

"Okay, who wants to go first," he'd say in a bored tone, which I always suspected was somewhat feigned.

In truth, I think he enjoyed being at the helm of this activity that he personally normally regarded as nothing more than a nuisance. Murray loved being in the lime-light regardless of the reason.

"Ahhh, that hurt!" I never seemed to get used to the stabbing pain the lancet caused to my finger as it jabbed in. "Okay, is that enough blood?" I'd ask as I pushed out a drop from my finger, placing it onto the test strip he held for me.

We'd always count down out loud as the numbers on his meter began descending, throwing out guesses as to what the resulting blood sugar count would be.

"Five point five!" we'd yell out in unison as the final figure appeared in the meter window.

"That's really good," he'd always inform me, we'd then move on to the next person in line.

My readings were always well within the range of normal, which starts at around four point five, and ends at about seven. We hadn't indulged in this activity for some time. If I asked him to bring out his blood glucose testing supplies for a good 'ol round of "Test your blood sugar," he told me that the batteries were dead and he was out of the testing strips.

Murray's physical appearance had begun to reflect his declining vitality. He was once again quite thin and his skin color had become uncharacteristically pale. Only a week prior I had casually commented to my mom that she shouldn't be surprised if Murray simply didn't wake up one morning. I certainly had no idea at that time just how eerily accurate and prophetic that statement would prove to be.

The doctors had informed us that an autopsy and investigation is routinely performed to determine cause of death. We were told that it could take up to three months to be completed. Four long months later we finally received the findings. The report stated that the presumed cause of death was low blood sugar. An absolute cause of death could not be given as Murray's blood sugar levels had not been tested until after he had been treated by the paramedics. In an effort to resuscitate him, he had been given glucose and epinephrine, which drastically altered his overall blood glucose reading. It wasn't a stretch to believe that hypoglycemia was in fact the cause of his death. On many previous occasions, Murray had told dramatic stories about incidents of low blood sugar that he had experienced upon waking. He described how if he hadn't willed himself out of bed to remedy the situation, he would have easily fallen into a diabetic coma. I always assumed Murray was exaggerating slightly when telling these stories. It appeared as though I'd been wrong.

From what we understood, Murray had already been lying dead for some time when Robin had tried to wake him that morning. If the report was accurate, Murray had likely taken his morning insulin shot at 6 a.m., and then returned to bed without ingesting enough calories to balance his glucose levels. I cannot help but ask myself if Murray would still be alive today, if only he had drank a bigger glass of orange juice that morning. I also can't help but wonder if his recent attempts to clean up his diet and decrease his beer consumption had actually backfired on him. I pondered just how a decrease in his overall calorie consumption could have contributed to his low blood sugar on that morning. The fact that he was not currently testing his levels would have meant he'd be unaware of a lower glucose reading that would have necessitated his need for less insulin. Unfortunately, these questions weren't answered by the autopsy, and being that Robin was asleep herself at the time, she couldn't provide any answers either.

In my communications with him since his death, I've asked him to provide clarity for me on this issue. I told that I wanted to know, "how he died."

He responded with a jovial, "Oh, you don't want to know. It's really not important anyway. The very fact that I died meant that it was my time to do so, that all was working as it should be.

Anytime now that the question of his cause of death comes into my mind, I can see his smiling face , again saying those words, "It's not at all important." I believe he doesn't want us to wring our hands over the fact that if he had only eaten or drank more after taking his shot, he'd still be alive. Still, on days when I'm really missing his physical presence, it's difficult not to ask these questions.

I had arranged to have the autopsy report mailed to me so as not to subject my parents to further distress. I opened my mailbox and recognized the envelope from the Medical Examiners Office. My heartbeat sped up. My hands became clammy.

I could barely read through the report for the tears blurring my eyes. It was excruciatingly difficult and somewhat surreal to read about my brother's body being dissected, examined, and mechanically commented upon by someone who was completely ignorant as to this uniquely wonderful person. When I finished reading, I was overcome with a fresh grief, and felt emotionally and physically drained. I sat at the table with my head in my hands, feeling like a limp dish-rag.

To distract myself, I began to sort through the other three pieces of mail that had arrived that day. My eyes widened when I realized that I was holding a pamphlet from the Canadian Diabetes Foundation. It struck me as an incredible coincidence that this piece of un-addressed mail should arrive in tandem with Murray's autopsy report. I grabbed another piece of mail. A pamphlet advertising a local residential painting company. Murray had owned and operated his own residential painting company at the time of his death. Inside the pamphlet was a picture of a painter, wearing a cap and overalls, who bore a strong resemblance to my brother. The trace of a smile came on my face and I began to get the tingly, light feeling that told me that Murray was once again communicating with me.

The final piece of mail was an envelope with several different offers inside. I couldn't open it fast enough, for I just knew beyond a shadow of a doubt that it would contain yet another reference to my brother. I had no idea just how uplifting this one would be. I sorted through the three advertisements inside and gasped loudly. An offer from the Bradford Exchange displayed a photo of a porcelain wall hanging that consisted of several strings of tiny porcelain angels. It was entitled "Heaven's Blessing." The hairs on the back of my neck stood up as a rush of loving energy surrounded me. I felt completely united and at one with my brother's spirit at that moment. Tears flowed down my cheeks, and I thanked Murray and the powers that be for providing me with these wonderful signs on such a difficult day.

Murray did not want me to feel sad and grieve for the life that he left behind, because he is now living in a place of peace and joy. It is a life free from pain, disease, and even the necessity to work at a boring job.

My heart felt light as I dried my tears. Somehow Murray had seen to it that the blow of receiving his autopsy report had been forever softened.

Chapter Fourteen

Electrical Communication

Since losing Murray, our family has developed a new appreciation of how precious our time is together. With this sentiment in mind, my husband announced that we should take a trip to Vancouver to visit Lori. We both suspected she was having a particularly difficult time managing her grief over Murray's death. She was living alone in Vancouver isolated from the rest of the family.

"Oh wow!" she exclaimed enthusiastically when we called to tell her of our plans. "It would be so great to see you guys."

"We thought we'd bring Jax along with us to celebrate his birthday. He'll be absolutely tickled at the thought of a plane ride and a visit to his auntie to celebrate his sixth birthday. We're going to surprise him with it," I told her.

"That is just perfect," she told me, obviously thrilled. "I'll book some time off work."

As we made plans for the trip, everything fell into place so perfectly that I felt sure Murray must have his hand in it.

The first night of our arrival, we gathered with close friends who had known and loved Murray. We spent a good part of the evening sharing our many memories. I also shared my stories of the numerous signs and messages I'd been receiving from him. Lori relayed a few signs of her own. It seemed that dragonflies had an uncanny knack of appearing around her whenever she was thinking of Murray.

It wasn't too long before we began discussing the possibility of Murray contacting us to say hello. "Where else would he be right now, if not here with all of us?" we joked.

"Okay, Murray," I addressed him out loud. "We want you to give us a really good sign while we're here in Vancouver. Maybe you could manipulate the lighting for us tonight."

We all sat in anticipation of flashing lights or a complete blackout. Nothing happened and we visited for the remainder of the evening without incident.

The following morning, Lori's phone rang. "Hi mom," I heard her say. Then, "Oh no, Oh my God, she's gone?" as she choked back tears. I realized immediately that mom was telling her that our Grandma had died. She had been ninety-one years old and had suffered a stroke a few weeks prior. We received the news with mixed emotions, sadness over losing our beloved Grandma, but also relief that her suffering was now over. Grandma had told me during a teary conversation immediately following Murray's death that she wanted to be with him. I had told her, "Grandma I absolutely know Murray will be there waiting for you when it's your time to cross over." There's no doubt in my mind that he greeted her with open arms when she made her transition.

Several hours later, we met with our friends from the previous evening at a nearby restaurant, to share brunch and share our sad news.

"Man, your poor dad must be having a rough time. First losing his son, and now his mother," our friend Dave commented emphatically, shortly after we had become seated.

Immediately the halogen light hanging directly over our table went out. We were all momentarily silenced.

"Oh my God, did you all see that?" I almost shouted.

"Unreal. Amazing." Everyone voiced their agreement, marveling over the incredible timing of this.

Our waitress had arrived at our table just as this transpired, and she too expressed her surprise. Our light was the only one out in the restaurant.

After much oohing and aahing, we had moved on to other conversation, when it came to our attention that the halogen light above our table was now slowly coming back on. We watched in silent fascination as it grew brighter and brighter, and then began to dim to its original radiance. Even Dave, a self-professed skeptic of anything supernatural, acknowledged that this was pretty incredible, particularly in light of our request to Murray on the previous night.

I truly believe that this was Murray and Grandma's way of letting us know that she had made her transition to the other side. They were now together, yet still both miraculously present in our lives.

Chapter Fifteen

It's Raining Poppies!

The arrival of spring brought with it a new realization of my loss. Murray had died during the winter, and now that everything in the physical world was coming back to life, it felt like Murray was left behind with the cold and the snow. It was difficult to feel happy anticipation about the warm weather and the promise of good times ahead, when I knew that Murray would not physically be a part of it.

"Oh my, what a beautiful morning," I said out loud as I gazed out my living room window." And yet, there I sat, feeling so dispirited I could hardly find the energy to move off of the couch.

"Hey mommy," Jax called as he skipped into the room. "Can we go bike riding?"

"Yeah, mommy, bike ride!" Iris chimed in, following behind him.

It was truly the last thing I felt like doing, but my children had been cooped up long enough with their melancholy mother. "Okay, guys, go get your helmets," I said with as much enthusiasm as I could muster. In a flurry of activity, we donned shoes and I buckled on their helmets. They exploded out the door, giggling with excitement as they headed towards their bikes.

As they happily rode towards the end of our street, I plodded aimlessly behind them, my thoughts on Murray. "Where are you buddy?" I silently asked him. "How come it feels like you're miles away?" I hadn't heard from him in awhile. He was probably just taking a well deserved break from my incessant requests.

As we approached the last house on our street, Jax's excited voice broke through my reverie. "Look what I found, mommy!" he called out. He bent down beside his bike to retrieve something from the grass.

"What do you have there sweetie?" I asked him, looking into his outstretched little hand. I could see he was holding a Remembrance Day lapel poppy. Murray had died on the morning of Remembrance Day. "Oh my god," was all I could say as I stared at it with awe. As I took the poppy from Jax's hand, I felt tears spring to my eyes as the familiar tingling feeling descended over me. Jax bent towards the grass again. This time he held up a lady bug, the first we had seen that spring. "Kids," I said my voice quivering, "Do you remember what day it is that we wear poppies?"

"Remembrance Day!" Jax was quick to answer.

"Well," I told him, "Uncle Murray died last Remembrance Day. Do you think that maybe this poppy could be his way of saying hello to us?" I asked. Both of their heads nodded in unison.

"And the lady bug too?" Iris inquired.

"You know, mommy, it was sitting right beside the poppy," Jax chimed.

"Yes, I think maybe Uncle Murray sent us the lady bug too," I told them, as I wiped tears from my eyes and smiled for the first time that day.

Jax was absolutely thrilled that he had been the one to find the sign from Murray this time and make mommy happy in the process.

When we arrived back home, I inspected the poppy. Even though it had likely been exposed to the elements since last November, it looked new. It was still bright red, its velvety texture in perfect condition. The black centre and the pin were missing, but I happily put it away in my jewelry box with my other keepsakes from Murray.

Three days later I was walking with Iris in her stroller to pick Jax up from kindergarten. Near the spot where we had found the poppy, I once again became filled with the sense of awe that I had originally felt upon finding it. "Imagine if I found another poppy in the same spot," I mused. I knew the chances were pretty remote, but still couldn't help enter-taining the idea. As I drew closer to the actual location, I caught sight of something red peeking out from the grass.

"It couldn't be!" I said out loud, my heart skipping a beat. Incredibly, another poppy lay in the exact same spot where Jax had found the first one. I entertained the possibility that perhaps someone was messing with me and had planted it there for me to find. But only Jax and Iris knew the precise location where we had found the first poppy. Somehow I just didn't think that they were capable of or interested in orchestrating such a hoax.

"Iris, look, another poppy," I gasped as I held the poppy up for her to see. My heart was pounding and I had tingles coursing through my body from head to toe.

Her eyes grew wide and she smiled brightly back at me. I pocketed the poppy and kept checking every few minutes to make sure it was still there. I didn't want to risk losing my proof.

As Jax ambled over to me as I stood outside the school doors where he exited kindergarten, I held the poppy up for him to see. "I found another one in the same spot!" I told him incredulously. "Murray sent us another poppy."

"Wow," was all he said, his eyes growing wide. He insisted on carrying it for me while we walked.

When I returned home, I immediately checked to see that the original poppy was still in its place, and sure enough it was. The newly found poppy looked exactly like the first—in great condition and missing the black centre and pin.

The next day as I was waiting in the school yard for Jax to come out of kindergarten, I began conversing with the father of one of his schoolmates. We began to discuss matters of a metaphysical nature, and my story of the poppies surfaced. He shared my amazement and then explained that he was infamous for finding items of value lying on the ground, in particular items that others were looking for.

When it was time to leave, we said our goodbyes and walked away. He soon called out to me and jogged over smiling.

"Here's the middle to your poppy," he said, opening his hand to reveal a tiny black poppy centre complete with the pin attached. For a second, time stood still. My mouth hung open as I stared blankly. Neither of us said anything, but I could sense by the expression on his face that he also realized we had just experienced a stunningly synchronistic event that could not be simply explained away as a mere coincidence. Spotting something so tiny lying in the grass was difficult enough to explain, but to have it happen on the heels of our conversation was something else entirely. I took the pin from him, thanking him profusely, and floated home with clouds under my feet. There seemed to be no limit to the lengths that Murray would go to in order to let me know that he was still an enduring presence in my life.

I believe that by providing me with a second poppy, Murray was addressing any tiny bit of doubt that I may have had. Undeniably, after finding the first poppy I was elated and felt quite sure that it was a sign from Murray, but the logical side of me had to admit that the element of chance still remained a possibility. However, the second poppy banished any logic. This was not coincidence. It would seem that Murray was intent upon convincing me of his communication, and went to yet further lengths by providing me with the centre and pin as further evidence.

A year later, Murray surprised me again. I was enjoying the warmth of the April sun on my morning run, when a vivid image of him popped into my head. At that precise moment, the distinctive call of a chickadee broke the silence. I slowed to a jog. "Is that you, Murray?" I wondered aloud, scanning the treetops. Another call came from overhead. "Okay Murray, if you're speaking to me through this bird, I want to hear the bird call again, on the count of three." I proceeded to count, "one, two....three." The same bird call echoed around me. I became infused with warmth and the tell-tale tingly feeling that confirmed that I had connected with my brother.

For no real reason, I averted my gaze from the view above me and looked down. There in front of me, mere inches from my foot, lay a Remembrance Day lapel poppy. If I hadn't looked downward at that precise moment I would have ran right overtop of it, never the wiser. Gingerly I picked it up. I had a lump in my chest and my eyes overflowed with tears. I felt completely surrounded by Murray's loving energy. I slowly got up and with an extra spring in my step, joyously resumed my run, poppy tightly in hand. I was so exhilarated, I felt like

I was flying!

When I arrived home, I excitedly told Eric and the kids about the bird calls and the subsequent find of another poppy. Eric commented that it was about the same time the previous year when I had found the first poppy. Anxious to confirm this, I consulted the journal where I keep notes on all my contacts with Murray. To my astonishment, it had been a year, minus a day. Without a doubt, I'll be expecting the appearance of another poppy next April!

About a month after this I was out for a night on the town with my girlfriend Marni. We were in high spirits as we had just shared an amazing meal and were headed to a pub to meet more friends. We were walking along the crowded street with a spring in our steps, engrossed in animated conversation, when Marni suddenly said "Let's ask Murray for a sign tonight."

I agreed and said, "Let's ask him to send us a poppy." I paused. "Well, maybe we shouldn't get so specific. He can send us whatever he wants."

We crossed the street and stepped up onto the curb. The store directly beside us caught my eye. "Oh my God, Marni, look!" I gasped as I grabbed her by the shoulder. Taking up almost the entire window front of an art store sat a painting of a flaming field of poppies. The timing had been absolutely perfect, right down to the second. We stood staring at this painting for several minutes with our mouths hanging open, surrounded by the magical feeling of tingling energy. We both sighed heavily. It was clear we both found it difficult to walk away from this incredibly timed and well placed painting, but eventually we agreed we had better get going. We slowly turned and walked away, both of us turning back for several more glances at the painting as we continued on our path. We remained awed by this experience for the remainder of the night.

I have since had the urge to resurrect some of my artistic leanings and decided to dig out my acrylic paints and brushes. Inspired by this painting of a poppy field, I decided to paint a tribute of sorts to my brother. The idea for the painting quickly took shape in my imagination; Murray flying over a field of bright red poppies into a purple sky containing a vortex of light, his guitar strapped onto his back and a six-pack of beer in his hands. Although I hadn't painted in years, the composition took shape on canvas almost miraculously. The poppy field came out exactly how I had pictured it, and my night-time sky came together with minimal effort.

When it came time to paint Murray's image, I hesitated. I've never been very good at depicting the human form. Past attempts have turned out quite awful and it was really important to me that I achieve some kind of a likeness to my brother. I decided I'd do better to create more of an impression of his form through the paint rather than an actual likeness. But when I put paint to canvas, I could suddenly feel Murray speaking to me, guiding me through it. "Make my butt look good," he joked as I painted his jeans. "Come on, fix up that cheek. I'm not a fat ass." I painted and laughed with my brother well into the wee hours of the morning, sipping red wine, oblivious to the passage of time.

Looking at my painting the next morning, I had to admit that I had managed to create a form that bore an uncanny resemblance to Murray. I should probably have signed Murray's name beside mine, since he guided me through it. The painting is now the focal point of my living room, and a constant reminder of my brother's newfound freedom.

Chapter Sixteen

An Angel on The Driveway?

About a year prior to Murray's death, Eric and I pulled up to my parents' house to see my brother's truck parked in their driveway.

"Oh yay, Murray's here!" I said happily, my heart giving a little leap. We pulled up to the driveway to park alongside his Truck. I hadn't seen Murray in a few weeks and couldn't wait to catch up with him and enjoy a good laugh or two.

"What the heck happened here?" Eric asked, as he got out of the car. We couldn't help but see that there were several large paint splatters directly underneath the back of Murray's truck hatch, staining the driveway concrete. Murray used his truck to carry painting supplies for his company.

"It looks like he dumped a can or two of paint doesn't it?" I said. "Is Dad ever going to freak." In the past my father had gotten severely bent out of shape over such things as small oil stains on his driveway. I recall being banned from parking on it at one point, when I had the misfortune of owning a car with an oil leak. I could only assume that a huge splatter of white and green paint would not exactly be considered an adornment to the properly.

Dad never made an issue over the spilled paint, much less ordered Murray to clean it up. In his own words, Dad wrote it off as mellowing with age. Nevertheless, it was very out of character for him to simply accept that kind of a mess.

Perhaps three months after Murray's passing, Eric and I were driving to my parents' house and I remembered the paint stain. I felt a strong urge that it would be formed into the shape of something significant. I could barely get out of the car fast enough to confirm this for myself. Part of the paint splatter appeared to be in the shape of an angel. I could decipher a head, a body formed by a flowing robe, and wings lying at the angel's sides. I asked my husband for his opinion, to make sure that I wasn't simply seeing what I wanted to see, and he readily agreed that he could also see the shape of an angel.

I raced inside to tell my parents that I had discovered an angel on their driveway, and I practically dragged them out to have a look.

"Oh yeah, I see it!" my mom told me excitedly. She pointed out the head, wings, and robe to my dad.

"I don't know," my dad answered, "If it were really an angel, wouldn't it have its wings up in the air? If this is an angel, then its wings are facing downwards."

"That is called nit-picking." I told him, smiling. "Always the skeptic," I added shaking my head.

Several weeks later, the angel shape appeared to have changed slightly. It seemed a fine white line had formed around its head, along with a blurring of the paint around the upper portion of the figure. It looked like a glowing halo.

There was another separate portion of the paint splatter shaped like a balloon, with a smaller balloon shape emanating from the top of it. Long before Murray's passing, I had used just such a diagram to illustrate how I viewed the spirit leaving the physical body. Was it possible that Murray was showing me through his paint splatter how his spirit left his body? Am I interpreting both of these paint splatters in light of what I would "like" to see in them? A spiritual "Rorschach test" of sorts? Perhaps it is a bit of both.

I believe that all of life's events are a reflection of that which we hope and ultimately believe we will see. Regardless, I allow myself to remain comforted by these paint splatters. Whenever I visit my parents, Murray's angel and his diagram of his spirit leaving his body greet me. I find it quite amazing that even after two years time, after enduring the harsh elements of sleet, rain, and snow, these images have retained their shape and clarity. There are times where I'd almost swear that they actually seem to grow brighter and more distinct. Who would have thought at the time that Murray's little "accident" would be so wonderfully uplifting for me?

Chapter Seventeen

A Group Effort

"Hey honey, do you want another beer?" I tried to yell loud enough to be heard over the music that was playing.

"Sure," Eric called back to me from the living room.

"Hey, save one for me too," I called out to Iris as I skipped into the living room to see that she and Eric were sharing a dance. He had her by both hands and much to her delight, was swinging her up in the air.

"Jax, care to join me?" I asked, grabbing him by the hand, and pulling him off the couch onto his feet.

"It's my turn to pick the next song," he sang out. "I want AC/CD!"

My husband, kids and I have adopted a tradition called family dance night. This generally occurs on a Friday or Saturday night, when Eric and I are feeling especially energetic, and possibly in the mood for a beer or two. On one of these evenings I had one of my most profound and direct communications with Murray.

We were all in naturally high spirits, taking turns playing our individual song selections and dancing exuberantly around the living room. I had cracked my second beer and was in a state of joyful celebration, very close to euphoria. While dancing with Jax, my thoughts drifted to Murray, as though guided by a beacon. He appeared in my mind's eye, clearer than at any other time.

"Oh wow!" I called out to Eric and the kids. "Murray's making contact! just give me a few minutes. I'll be upstairs." I immediately cut my dance short and grabbed a pen and paper. I disappeared up to my bedroom to concentrate on Murray's voice and record as much as I could, as accurately as I could.

I sensed that he was with a group of male comrades, possibly family or friends, and it seemed that they were having a party of sorts of their own. Boisterous laughter and excited conversation swirled around

Murray. I felt the exuberance and lightheartedness of their collective mood, along with an eagerness to communicate with me. Everyone seemed intent on adding their own voice to the exchange that Murray and I were having.

"Where are you Murray?" I asked out loud. "What's it like?"

He responded with passion and enthusiasm. I remembered the special connection we had as children, the way we could simply look at one another and we'd know what the other was thinking. I could clearly see his face in my mind's eye, filled with excitement, his eyes registering his intense desire to make me understand the magnitude and validity of what he was conveying to me. "It's f-ing real, Faye!" he told me over and over. "It's a real place, and it's more f-ing amazing and incredible than you could ever imagine. I have a real life here, complete with real activities. I'm busy, I'm involved, I'm having fun. You'll understand better what I'm describing when you get here, but until then, just know that life after death really does exist. I'm still alive and I'm happier than I've ever been."

Words cannot explain just how vivid and real this communication was to me, or how close I felt to Murray during this exchange. He was the same old Murray, complete with the use of profanity to express himself. So much for previous notions I may have had about spirit becoming automatically sanctimonious or holy when it leaves the physical plane.

He went on to explain that he is available to speak with me anytime. "In most cases," he told me. "You are not nearly "high" enough in vibration for us to connect. Direct contact is only possible during times that our vibrations are close to the same frequency. Your vibrational state at this time is high enough for you to hear me." He conveyed to me that when this direct contact is not possible, he is still as close as can be and that he communicates with me using other methods, such as the signs that I had been picking up. His message was conveyed to me both through his actual words, which I heard inside of my head, as well as through thoughts or concepts that I interpreted telepathically. Throughout it all, a visual of his smiling face remained in the forefront of my mind.

He and the others, whom I wasn't able to tune into deeply enough to fully recognize individually, began to supply information about our existence in general. They explained that one lifetime is merely a very short cycle completed within an eternity of cycles. We can never be separated from those that we love because they continue to cycle and evolve along with us in this never-ending dance of life. We are eternally connected by our love for one another; therefore, there is never really any separation. In each physical lifetime, we come into this world to take on varying roles in relation to our loved ones from past lives. They referred to these souls who go through the reincarnational cycle again and again together as members of a 'soul family.' I could sense laughter and unrestrained excitement and joy amidst the presentation of this information. Murray wanted me to know that he was still with me and always would be; there was no sense grieving his death.

At one point in our conversation, Iris called out to me from behind my closed door, in an angry, demanding voice, "Mommy, let me in. Let me in now. I want you!"

Murray joked, "she's a bit of a brat, isn't she?" In my mind's eye, I could see his eyebrows raised, a huge smile on his face. I couldn't help but laugh.

As they all began to say goodbye, I thanked them and returned to my family to resume our dancing. I was so empowered with an abundance of vibrant energy that I barely stopped for the next three hours. I felt like I was floating on a cloud of joy. Eric and I discussed the experience I had just had, and in between dance moves, we philosophized like crazy, solving all the mysteries of the universe in one night's work. Once again, I acknowledged how lucky I was to have a husband who was so open to all of this, and who never once questioned the validity of these experiences I was having.

When I finally felt tired enough to go to bed, I let out a deep sigh, as I envisioned how tired I'd likely be the next day. For a parent of two young children, there is rarely such a thing as a day off. In spite of their later than usual bedtime, our little ones would likely be up before 7 a.m.

As I began to drift off to sleep, I asked Murray to help me to keep my energy high, so I wouldn't have to suffer with fatigue the next day.

When I woke up the next morning, I was absolutely overflowing with an abundance of energy and positive feelings. In fact, I don't ever recall having a day that was filled with such pure joy. I felt euphoric and had an overall uplifted perspective on life that lasted for several days afterwards.

This memory has continued to serve as a powerful example to me of where I need to be energetically or vibrationally in order to connect in this direct way with my brother. I've learned that in most instances, this type of euphoric, sky-high vibration must be achieved incrementally. Rarely does it come upon me and last for such a length of time as it did on this particular evening. Reaching a place where I can converse in this direct way with Murray is usually a result of slow but steady, peaceful, elevated thought choices over a period of time.

I cherish every direct contact with my brother and honour it as the miracle that it is, while I continue to remain grateful for the more subtle interactions with him that fill up the spaces between.

Chapter Eighteen

A Dream Meeting

I've had numerous dreams about Murray since his passing. Most mornings, I recall having had at least one dream about Murray during the night. However, most of these dreams do not contain the element of reality that indicates that I've truly been connecting with him. These dreams are pleasant in the sense that Murray is a part of their content, but they leave me feeling somewhat disappointed. They are the mere equivalent of thinking about spending time with him.

Almost seven months after his death I had an especially vivid dream. It was so real that it left me with an unshakeable knowing that I had connected with Murray in another reality.

While sleeping and dreaming, I entered into a state of lucidity where I suddenly became conscious of the fact that I was dreaming. "Okay, here I am," I said to myself. "Awake in a dream. I better make the most of it before I wake up. What should I do? Oh wow, maybe I can visit with Murray."

Within the dream I willed myself to the top of the stairway in my home, which has a view out of the front door window. I saw Murray's green truck pull up in front of our house. He opened the driver's side door, got out, and walked up the front steps towards the door. I was overcome with anticipation as I realized that it was really my brother coming up my front steps! I floated down the stairs, heading towards the door to greet him. The moment that he came through the door, I grabbed him, hugging him as hard as I could, and broke into tears. "Oh Murray, I miss you so much. Do you have any idea how hard this had been? Oh God, I hope you've known all this time how much you mean to me and how much I love you," I told him.

He responded without words, but telepathically I picked up his emotions of love and joy, and his acknowledgement of all I had felt and experienced since his death. He hugged me back tightly. Neither of us spoke further or felt the need to. We conveyed it all through our embrace. This went on for several blissful minutes until my waking mind began to intrude.

Upon waking, I felt ecstatic that I had just spent time with Murray. The few precious moments that we had been together were undeniably real. This was not "just a dream." The emotions involved were far too intense.

Groggy from sleep, I turned on the TV in my bedroom to entertain myself while I performed some morning exercises. The TV screen showed large white letters reading, "You are not dreaming." My eyes instantly opened wide as a jolt of adrenaline shot through me. These words it seemed, were for my eyes only, a message to reassure me that my dream was real. I quickly realized they were actually the new slogan for a soft drink commercial. It was extremely interesting timing.

I couldn't get this dream out of my mind for the rest of the day. I stood in the exact spot in my living room where our encounter had taken place. The whole scene in its entirety came flooding back to me, complete with all the heart-wrenching emotions. I sank to my knees in tears, as I recalled how wonderful it had felt to come physically face-to-face with Murray. This was the first communication where I had felt that I had made physical as well as emotional contact with Murray, and the impact of it was awesome. I felt healed and very peaceful for some time afterwards. Nearly two years since experiencing this dream, I can still recall the minute details of it as vividly as if I had dreamed them last night.

Chapter Nineteen

Murray the Crow

The crow that became known to our family as "Murray," made his first appearance in the green space in front of our home shortly after my brother's death.

"Mommy, there's that black bird again," Jax called out as he pointed in the direction of a big black crow. "Look, he's coming closer." It seemed whenever I was buckling the kids into their car seats in preparation for an outing, this crow would strut out onto the road, drawing up next to the car, making his presence known by walking in circles and cawing loudly.

"He sure seems to like us doesn't he?" I replied, laughing. "Maybe this bird is somehow connected to Murray," I thought to myself.

As I buckled myself in and pulled away from the curb, the crow continued to sit on the sidewalk. As I turned onto the main road that ran on the adjacent side of the green space in front of our home, this crow followed us by swooping over it and landing by the side of the road, mere feet away from the car as we drove by. "Wow," I told the kids, "that crow really seems to want our attention."

I cannot count how many times while returning home, I turned left onto the street that connects with ours, only to have this crow fly directly in front of the car windshield, dangerously close, and then soar up into the tree on the corner. Whenever I started off on my morning jog, he'd perch high up on top of the first streetlight along my path, cawing loudly as though he was cheering me on as I passed underneath. If he was in fact trying to get my attention, he was doing a fine job.

After several weeks of observing this bird's behavior I announced to Eric and the kids, "I think we should call the crow Murray." The name stuck.

One afternoon while I was working on this book, it dawned on me that I hadn't received a sign from my brother for several weeks. I took a short break from writing and mentally asked him to send me a message as soon as possible. Fifteen minutes later, Eric and the kids came in, rosy-cheeked, and all smiles after a trip to the park. "Mommy, Mommy, look what I have for you," Iris called out to me as she came running towards me. She brought her little hand out from behind her back, holding a big black feather. As it had been this precise chapter on "Murray the Crow" that I had been working on at that time, her find could not have been more perfectly timed. I was quite certain that once again, Murray had provided me with my requested sign.

The next day, quite by accident, I came upon a Native American Zodiac website. On a whim, I casually scrolled down to Murray's birth date of October 16. I was stunned to see that his sign was none other than that of the black crow. I found this to be an interesting and significant parallel. It further confirmed for me that this crow who had entered our lives had ties to Murray.

At one point during the summer, the crow and possibly some of his buddies had seen fit to defecate all over our car. There was so much bird poop that it truly looked as though someone had thrown a couple of buckets of white paint all over the car. If I didn't know better, I would have thought that we were the brunt of a practical joke. Perhaps we had been. This type of stunt would be right in keeping with Murray's sense of humor. Perhaps not quite what one might expect from an encounter with the divine, but I've come to see that spirit often works in surprising ways.

Around mid-summer, Murray the crow was joined by a smaller black crow. Our assumption that this was his mate was confirmed one afternoon by the appearance of a baby crow in my flower bed. At the time, I was quietly reading a book, seated on the couch directly in front of the floor-to-ceiling living room window, when I heard a terrible ruckus going on directly outside. The two adult crows were cawing loudly. I looked down into the flower bed and saw a baby crow hopping frantically about with frightened movements, obviously unable to fly. My initial response of pleasant surprise was quickly overtaken by panic, as I realized that my three cats were presently outside in the back yard. I knew that if they came upon this baby, he wouldn't stand a chance. I quickly ran out the front door. Both crow parents protested loudly and menacingly swooped down at me as I headed towards the baby crow. I caught him in both of my hands as he was about to hop under a bush. I rushed him across the street into the green space. He bit my hands repeatedly, as he struggled in an attempt to escape, poor little thing. I placed him as high up as I could reach on the branch of an evergreen tree. The adult crows had followed me to the green space in an effort to protect their youngster.

For the remainder of the day, I kept my cats inside and made periodic checks to see that the baby crow was still on his perch. Right up until darkness fell, I could see him sitting still and solitary on the tree branch. In the morning he was gone. I optimistically told myself that he probably had perfected his flying skills and had sailed off into the early morning sky.

A day later, I discovered his half-eaten body lying in the grass in the green space, several feet from the tree that he had been perched in. Several yards away I found what appeared to be the lifeless body of his brother or sister lying in the grass. The two adult crows were circling overhead, cawing loudly. They both disappeared several days later, leaving me feeling heavy hearted and confused over the whole incident.

Several weeks later, the kids and I visited friends who live about two miles from our home. As I was buckling the kids into the backseat, a large black crow began making an incredibly noisy ruckus. I turned around to see it perched on top of a fence about eight feet directly behind me. The crow sounded extremely agitated and aggressive, cawing mightily until I got into the car. As I began to drive away, I glanced out of my side window. The crow was flying directly beside the car at the exact height as my window, less than two feet from my face. He continued to do so for several surreal moments before veering off.

The kids and I speculated over whether or not this could be the same crow that we had come to know as Murray. I guess we'll never know for sure, but this particular crow certainly seemed to have something important to say to us.

We live in a lake community within the city. During the summer I'd often take the kids to the beach to play in the sand while I worked on this book. One sunny afternoon, I was sitting on a picnic bench diligently reviewing my writing. Out of nowhere a seagull came soaring up and past me, flying so close that it actually brushed my cheek with the tip of its wing. I placed my hand against my cheek where the bird's wing had touched me, as a rush of loving energy surrounded me. Once again, I was working on this chapter. I strongly suspect that this was Murray's way of validating its content.

Chapter Twenty

Murray's Humor..... Alive and Well!

"We're nothing more than a flea on a dog's ass! God's probably having a real good laugh at us all." Murray laughed heartily, before having a quick swig of his beer.

"What about the whole heaven and hell thing?" I asked him. We were engaging in one of our regular conversations about the meaning of life.

"Hell? what a joke that is," he replied, smirking. "Nobody's going to hell when they die. This right here, is hell." He said as gestured into the air emphatically with his pointer finger. "I don't know about you but I'm actually looking forward to the experience of the afterlife once this body of mine finally gives out."

"Oh I'm sure you have a few good years left," I told him, raising my beer in the air. You know what they say, only the good die young." I giggled as he rolled his eyes in mock exasperation.

"The truth is, I don't mind if I cut out early. Who in their right mind would want to live to get old and withered? Nope, no adult diapers for me, I'm hoping to leave before I start the downhill slide. Take me, take me to a better place." he said as he looked longing up to the ceiling, a big goofy grin on his face.

I miss Murray's sense of humor most of all. I had always eagerly anticipated the funny and often inappropriate material that would come flowing forth from him. You never really knew what Murray would say or do. He could freak out the squeamish easily, but he also had no trouble mentally scarring those of us more accustomed to his socially-and-politically-incorrect musings. There was no doubt that crossing over the line into "poor taste territory" was Murray's forte. Therefore, it really shouldn't have surprised me at all when he began laying some really morbid, tasteless jokes on me after his death. Certainly, joking about his own loss of life would not be out of the realm of Murray's wild sense of humor.

He and I both used our birthdays to playfully rib each other about our physical mortality. On his 33rd birthday, I chose a card undeniably morbid and inappropriate. I knew Murray would love it. It depicted the grim reaper, arm outstretched, beckoning with his bony finger. The caption read "That's right, come to Papa." We both had a huge laugh when I presented it to him. It comforts me now to know that Murray took such a lighthearted approach to the subject of death.

Eight years later, about a month prior to Murray's passing, I once again poured over greeting cards at a gift shop, coming dangerously close to choosing another card of similar content. This one depicted a man driving a car and an image of the grim reaper in his rearview mirror. The caption read "Objects in this mirror may be closer than they appear." Intuition told me that this might be hitting a bit close to home on this particular birthday. With a strange feeling of foreboding in my gut, I put it down.

Instead I chose a humorous, lighthearted card depicting two hillbilly siblings representative of Murray and me. The near toothless boy was blindfolded, hitting a piñata that was actually a bag of rotting garbage tied up to a tree branch. His equally dentally-challenged sister, encouraged him with the caption, "Whoo-wee, whack it a good 'un, Cleetus!" He absolutely loved this card, and for the entire month afterwards, right up until the day before his passing, Murray and I would banter this phrase back and forth at one another during visits and phone conversations. Murray even apparently started playfully calling his girlfriend "Cleetus." I remain forever thankful that I declined to choose the grim reaper card. Whether Murray would have found it funny or not, I'm sure it would have haunted me forever. Mocking my brother's death one month before it actually transpired would have been going over the top. In light of all the fun we had with the hillbilly card, I think I can rest assured that I made the right decision.

Prior to Murray being diagnosed with diabetes, he had dropped over twenty pounds from his already slender frame. A very close friend of ours, another by the name of "Marnie," who was Murray's high school sweetheart, also possessed a wild sense of humor. She had tagged him with the nickname "Bones." She would often pipe up with a litany of "clickety-clackety, clickety-clackety," when Murray would enter the room. He'd have a little chuckle along with us, but I could tell by his restrained laugh and the way he averted his eyes, that on some level it bothered him. It may have actually been one of the things that prompted him to seek medical attention. I believe that this was partly Marnie's intent, as at this time Murray was in deep denial that he had a health problem. Long after Murray had been properly diagnosed and had regained his original weight, the nickname Bones surfaced when the three of us were together. Because his extreme thinness was no longer an issue, he laughed heartily right along with us.

While out shopping several months after his death, I decided to look for a silk scarf or fabric bag to enclose Murray's ashes in before placing them in the urn that I had chosen. My eye was attracted by a black and white patterned scarf. I was momentarily disturbed to see that the scarf was patterned with a tiny skull and crossbones motif. No, too inappropriate, I thought. Then I felt laughter and that unmistakable feeling that Murray was near. I couldn't find a fabric bag and all of the other scarves on display were also unsuitable for less disturbing reasons. I left the store empty-handed and strongly sensing Murray's presence.

I drove directly over to my parents' place to see if my mom had anything suitable for Murray's ashes. I followed her into the spare room where she began rummaging around in a drawer. "How about this?" she said as she pulled a drawstring bag from the dresser drawer. It was made out of black fabric and to my utter disbelief, when I turned it over I saw that it had a large white skull and crossbones printed on it! Neither of us could recall ever having seen this bag before, but we both agreed that it had probably come from a pirate toy set of Jax's. All I knew was that it was my second coincidental run-in with the skull and crossbones theme that afternoon.

Later, while describing these occurrences to a friend, she commented that if Murray was responsible for them, then possibly there was a message inherent in them. We came to the conclusion that Murray probably wanted me to keep things light, that even his death could be a joking matter, and that most of all he was still around helping me to see the lighter side of things. I surmised that he was joking about his own death and making reference to his nickname of "Bones" at the same time. I have not yet put his ashes into the skull and crossbones bag, but I'm not completely ruling it out either. I'm sure that I have far more of a problem with it than Murray ever would.

Christmas 2006 was more difficult for all of us than the previous year which came a mere month after Murray's death. At that time we were still reeling from the extreme shock of it all, and were therefore somewhat numbed to our various emotions. Now it was incredibly evident, by the scant amount of laughter and joking, that Murray was physically absent from our festivities. Christmas just wasn't Christmas without Murray around. We had grown to rely on him for his exuberance and sense of fun, as he always provided us with much comic relief. The void of his absence was felt by all. He was on my mind constantly.

As I entered my parents' dining room on Christmas Day, my eyes fell upon the red Christmas party crackers lying on the dinner plates. I recalled a friend's story about receiving a compelling sign from her daughter's spirit on the first Christmas after her passing. She had pulled apart a Christmas cracker and found an extremely significant and relevant object inside. I had an instant knowing that I would also be receiving a sign from Murray through the trinket that I'd find inside my cracker. I didn't know where I'd be sitting, so I silently wondered which cracker would be mine.

Shortly thereafter, Jax chose a seat for himself, and firmly informed me that I was sitting next to him. He even grabbed the cracker off the plate and waved it under my nose. "Okay then, Murray, this is it," I thought. Everyone began pulling apart their crackers. Anticipation rose within me. Jax grabbed one end of my cracker and I grabbed the other. We pulled it apart, making a loud and satisfying "pop." Out fell a red party hat. A good sign I thought, as I happened to be wearing a red sweater. "Always a good thing to coordinate the accessories," I mused. I had to dig inside the remaining cardboard tube to retrieve my prize. I laughed out loud. Gracing the palm of my hand was a tiny, yellow, plastic skeleton. I had received the sign that I had been asking for. Once again it seemed that Murray was using his special brand of humor to joke with me from the other side. Out of all fourteen crackers, most contained charm-like items that were very similar to each other. Mine was the only one containing a skeleton. Little "Bones" is now clickety-clacketying next to my poppies, guitar pick, and other Murray keepsakes.

These tangible items serve as "solid" proof that Murray is communicating with me, but his telepathic communications are just as reliable. These communications occur as fleeting thoughts, different enough from my own that I know to accept them as communications from Murray. Admittedly, a certain element of faith and trust are necessary when interpreting and ultimately accepting these messages as originating with Murray. The signs and telepathic messages are always accompanied by a state of incredible emotional well-being, tingling up my spine and a feeling of expanded consciousness, which I now recognize as my barometer indicating Murray's presence.

One afternoon while driving down a side street, I received the following unmistakable telepathic "hello" from my brother. I began to approach a house with a tree in front with a white rope hanging from one of the branches. As I passed in front of the house, the wind blew the rope forward. I received a clear picture in my mind's eye of Murray clinging to the rope with a huge goofy smile plastered to his face. I laughed heartily and felt his love and humor surrounding me. To this day, I can still see this image clearly and it continues to make me smile.

I cannot count the many times that Murray's voice pops into my head in response to something that is going on in my life. He often makes an off-color joke of some sort, assuring me of his presence at that moment. In some ways I am closer now to my brother than I have ever been. It seems that in his newfound form of spirit, he is merely a thought away.

Chapter Twenty-One

Murray's Birthday

Life is self affirming in its continuous push forward. While the passage of time eases the feelings of shock and powerful grief that initially accompanied my brother's death, I find myself wanting to slow it down. Each month that passes takes me farther away from the last time I was in Murray's physical presence. I miss him immensely, and all the signs and messages from him cannot erase that fact.

October sixteenth. Had Murray been alive, he would have turned forty-two today. We enjoyed sharing the same numerical age for the two month period leading up to my birthday in December. This was the first year in my life that I wasn't sharing this with Murray, and it left a huge void.

I looked out the window at the swirling, heavy falling snow. It seemed fitting. The skies were acknowledging this as a special day by releasing their white fluffy confetti for the first time this season. "Time for school Jax!" I called out.

"Do we get to wear our snow-pants today?" He asked excitedly

"Yes, you and Iris get to wear your snow-pants, and we're taking the sled." I informed them.

"Yay! I get to ride on the sled!" Iris cheered.

We all bundled up into our winter clothes and headed out into the snow. As I trudged across the school field, the two of them reminded me that snow can be so much more than a wet and cold inconvenience. They alternated between riding in the sled and rolling out of it. They tried to make snow balls out of the fluffy snow, then threw the white powdery puffs at each other. They frolicked the entire way, almost making Jax late for class. By the time Iris and I returned to the house, I was reveling in the beauty of the fluffy snowflakes that drifted down from the heavens. I stood in front of our house, head tilted upwards. Warm tears rolled silently down my icy cheeks. Iris was in her own happy little world, making snow angels completely oblivious to me. I could feel Murray close by, in my gratitude for that moment and maybe even in the snow itself. Will he acknowledge his birthday with a sign for me? I wondered.

I'm convinced that I received my answer several hours later when I reached into my mailbox. I pulled out a single envelope addressed to me. It was from the same woman who sent me the butterfly envelope the previous winter. Once again this client of mine had sent me payment enclosed within a beautiful card that she had thoughtfully left unsigned so that I could make use of it myself at a later date.

I opened the envelope in high expectation. I gasped aloud as I pulled out a card with a picture of a winter fairy riding a white horse in a snow storm on the front of it. Inside was a picture of a black feather and the inscription, "Sending you Light and Love." This had to be a message from Murray. The black feather was in keeping with his communications involving the black crow, and the winter fairy riding in a snow storm was a wonderful representation of my experience in the snow that morning. This was the second time Murray had sent me a message through this client. On both of these occasions, it had been snowing outside. This woman was unaware of my brother's upcoming birthday or of the signs that I had been receiving from him, but she was certainly thrilled when I later told her of the part she had played in helping me to feel my brother's presence.

We celebrated Murray's birthday later that day, as a family, by having dinner at his favorite Japanese restaurant. This had long ago been established as Murray's birthday ritual, and we had no plans to end it. In spite of his absence, we enjoyed our meal, with minimal tears and lots of reminiscing. I felt quite sure that he was near, enjoying the festivities and laughing along with us.

This is one of several traditions we've established as a means to continue to celebrate the important dates in Murray's life. We're all finding that these little rituals are extremely helpful in the process of moving forward, while continuing to keep us feeling connected to Murray. It really helps to know that although our memories of him reside in the past, he's still going to continue to be a significant and integral part of our future.

Chapter Twenty-Two

Spotting a Look-Alike

Nothing quite takes my breath away these days like catching a glimpse of someone who resembles my brother. Murray had taken to wearing a backwards baseball cap during the last five years of his life. More than a mere fashion statement, it was a means to cover up a thinning head of hair. Years previous, he had enjoyed a luxurious, thick crop that he had worn long and elaborately styled. His hair had been one of his defining physical attributes, and as he began to thin out on top, I think he felt as though he was losing a part of himself. The cap became his new signature and he was rarely seen without it.

The mere glimpse of someone wearing a backwards cap has the potential to make my heart leap. Fleeting sightings of those who are off in the distance affect me the most. It's far easier for my imagination to fill in the blanks and "create my brother." In that moment I can almost convince myself that I am watching my brother in the flesh, and it makes me feel the physical closeness to him that I've been craving since his death.

One late sunny afternoon, Eric, the kids and I had just pulled up to a strip mall, with plans to have dinner at a restaurant located several doors down. The business directly in front of us was a 'Money Mart', a business that cashes cheques for a fee. Laborers were coming and going at a steady rate, many of them wearing work caps and clothing similar to Murray's.

"Okay, Eric, am I crazy or does that guy up at the counter look a whole lot like Murray?" I asked my husband as I gazed out of the car windshield.

"Yeah, Eric agreed, as he squinted slightly and moved closer to the windshield to get a better look. "He does look like Murray. Let's see if he'll turn around."

"Look he's even standing and moving like Murray. Remember how he used to rock back and forth like that when he felt impatient?" I said, my eyes filling with tears. This man at the counter wore his cap backwards and had his hands in his front pockets. He was casually rocking back and forth, a typical Murray mannerism. The front window of the business was partially covered by shadow. I could almost believe that I was viewing the back of my brother. I squelched the urge to run inside and confront this person. As we exited the car, I couldn't take my eyes off him.

As I took a few steps forward, the light shifted, removing the shadow from the window and breaking the spell. "Oh my God," I said, "He looks absolutely nothing like Murray." The person that I was now looking at could not look anything less like my brother. He was far shorter, with a much larger build, and his clothing was actually unlike anything that Murray would have worn.

"No, you're right he doesn't even resemble Murray," Eric agreed, chuckling.

I was about to continue on to the restaurant when this man we had been watching, turned his head and looked directly at me. His face was also completely different from Murray's, but in the next instant his eyes began to shine with a bright light. In the next instant, they appeared to become my brother's eyes. I stared back in disbelief, as I gasped out loud. His face continued to remain his own, while the eyes of my brother glowed brightly, shining their light into mine. I suddenly realized, this person was probably wondering why this crazy lady was staring at him so intently. After several seconds of open-mouthed gawking, I averted my gaze. I began crying. "Did you see his eyes?" I asked Eric. "I saw Murray's eyes glowing in his face."

"There did seem to be a strange glow coming from eyes," Eric agreed. "I saw it too. Maybe it was the way the sun was shining through the window," he suggested.

"Maybe," I responded through my tears. "But that still wouldn't explain why I saw Murray's eyes."

I can't help but question just exactly what transpired on that day. Even so, I will never forget how my brother's eyes burrowed into me. This was certainly the most "metaphysical" of all of the signs that I have received from Murray to date.

I've asked Murray many times to appear to me in visible form. I think he would do it if he thought that I could handle it emotionally. His exact words regarding this subject are, "I don't want to mess ya up!" I wonder if my response to the glowing eyes convinced him that I can handle a full visual manifestation of his spirit. I kind of think not. I'll keep working on it, Murr, I promise!

Chapter Twenty-Three

Messages by Moonlight

Almost a year after Murray's passing, I had what I believe to be a late night visit from him. I was deep in sleep, dreaming, and I had an awareness of Murray being present with me, as though the two of us were sharing one mind, dreaming in tandem. The dream itself had nothing to do with Murray.

"Swish-swish-gurgle," I became aware of a sound occurring in my physical reality, outside of my dream, from somewhere in the house. I began to wake up. As I slowly became conscious, I could hear that this sound was coming from the bathroom. It was the toy fishing rod that the kids played with in the bathtub. It had a button on the handle that activated a loud, and rather annoying sound of moving water.

"Swish-swish-gurgle," the fishing rod sounded again. I reluctantly opened my eyes. "I suppose I'm the one who's going to have to get up and turn this thing off. Man, can't anyone else hear that?" I queried out loud. I felt irritated at having my sleep interrupted.

It suddenly occurred to me that Murray had caused this toy to activate, as a way of letting me know that he had really been with me while I dreamed. "Yes, I told myself," nodding my head. It's Murray alright." Instantly, I could feel him telepathically confirming this for me.

I had just stepped onto the bathroom floor with my second foot when the toy stopped making its noise. "I can feel you right here Murray," I mumbled to myself. I thought I might actually bump into an apparition of him, I was that certain of his presence. I quickly acknowledged that at that moment I wasn't prepared to encounter a physical manifestation of his spirit. Ironic, and rather humorous since I spend a great deal of time hoping and praying for him to appear to me in a visible form. Despite the strong feeling of his presence, I returned to bed without incident, and the fishing rod has stayed quiet ever since.

Several days after this occurrence, I found myself deep in thought about the nature of our consciousness once we leave this earthly plane. Amongst the many questions that I had, one in particular was causing me a great deal of thought. Do we retain the fullness of our distinct personalities or do we become somewhat merged with the oneness of all things? My previous communications with Murray certainly led me to believe that he was still the same person, but I had recently encountered differing views on this subject and was desiring some clarification. Murray seemed to be communicating to me that both scenarios are true. Although he had retained his identity and could focus solely upon it, he could somehow also simultaneously expand and broaden his perspective, thus experience the totality of his spirit. This was a concept that confused me and I seemed to be having difficulty making a strong enough connection with Murray on this subject, to completely understand what he was attempting to convey. In short, I really desired to know if the spirit of Murray that I was communicating with was the same Murray that I had known and loved when he'd been alive.

Prior to sleep, I asked Murray to send me an answer in the form of a dream. Upon waking the next morning, I had a clear recollection of the following dream:

A girl that I met at a social gathering agreed to swap bodies with me for a short period of time. As I found myself inside of her body, I acknowledged how different it felt physically. I ran my hands over my new body parts, in wonder over my temporary new self, noting the various differences between this body and my own. I realized I was still completely myself. Exchanging bodies had not changed my personality or who I was at the core of my being. It had merely altered my perspective somewhat.

I believe this dream gave me the answer that I had been looking for. Changing form does not change who we really are. While Murray is now certainly in a different form and has gained a broader perspective, the personality I know as Murray still exists and will always be available to me. This dream has comforted me and has strongly reinforced that the most reliable answers lie within. All we need to do is ask.

Chapter Twenty-Four

Murray's Ashes

"While I'm here, I think it's time we divided up Murray's ashes, what do you guys think?" My sister Lori asked. Eric and I were driving her back to our place after picking her up from the airport as she had just flown in for a visit from Vancouver. "I think it's high time," she added.

"Yes," I agreed. "I think we've put it off for long enough. Lord knows it's going to be hard. I think we've all been trying to avoid this, particularly mom and dad. But poor Murray, well.. his ashes anyway, have been sitting in that box in their closet for over a year now. Yeah," I told her. "It's time." Our family had decided that after Murray's cremation, we would divide his ashes amongst us. We had all deliberately delayed this task.

Lori and I prepared for the event at my parents' house by laying a purple table cloth over the dining room table. "Mom," I called out. "Could you grab a couple of your favorite photos of Murray? I'll find some candles." We all gathered our individual urns along with small plastic bags for each and placed them on the table.

"Look everyone," Jax proudly held up a crystal bell he had found inside my mom's curio cabinet. "Can we use this?" he inquired. The bell had been engraved with "The Lord is my Shepherd" prayer.

"That bell belonged to your great-great grandma," my mom told him. We all agreed that it was quite fitting to use in our ceremony.

Mom, Dad, Lori, Eric, the kids and I sat around the living room, looking at photos and tearfully reminiscing about our many memories of Murray. "Man, he was a good looking dude, wasn't he?" I exclaimed. "Oh I wish so much I could sit across from him again and listen to one of his crazy stories," I said, sniffing back tears.

"Yes," mom agreed, "He was quite the character alright."

"I hope he gives us some kind of sign that he's here with us tonight," Lori added.

"I can feel him here already," I told her.

Lori noted a perfect full moon in the clear night sky, to grace our ceremony. We waited several hours before progressing until the moment felt absolutely perfect. We dimmed the dining room chandelier, lit the candles, and put on some of Murray's favourite music.

As we all gathered around the table, the chandelier lights began to dim and then brighten again in intensity. Almost in unison, the fluorescent lights in the adjacent kitchen also began to flicker.

"Wow," I said, "The air feels absolutely thick with Murray's presence. Can you all feel it too?" Lori, my mom and Eric all nodded in agreement, as they wiped tears from their eyes.

At Jax's urging, we took turns ringing the crystal bell and then I opened up the bag inside of the box that contained Murray's ashes. I immediately began crying hard as I looked inside to see what remained of my brother's body.

"Oh God, I cried, it looks like there are pieces of bone in the ash and feel how heavy this bag is. I really didn't think there'd be so much ash." The full realization that this was all that remained of Murray's physicality hit us all hard.

Through our tears, we took turns scooping ashes into a plastic bag, which we then placed inside our individual urns. "Okay mom, you can go first," I told her. We watched silently as she pursed her lips and quickly and precisely scooped her ashes into her plastic bag, zipped it shut, dropped it into her urn, and crisply snapped the lid on top. Eric, Lori, and I burst into laughter in response.

"Good lord Mom, such efficiency!" Lori commented, giggling. The mood was immediately lightened and Murray's presence could be felt stronger than ever.

I scooped my ashes into a plastic zip-lock bag. "Murray would have found this hysterical you know," I told everyone as I smiled through my tears at his various probable responses.

"Take lots now," my mom encouraged, as though I was helping myself to a bowl of mashed potatoes at a family dinner. We all laughed. "Now, don't be shy girls, dig deep!" I tried to mimic Murray. The lights continued to flicker and dance overhead.

We had all finished scooping our ashes and stood around the table talking when Iris interrupted us. "Look," she exclaimed exuberantly, displaying her hands. She had been playing with the scoop we had used and her tiny hands were covered in black ash.

"Oh no," I exclaimed, my hands flying to my chest. "She's even got it all over her face and pajamas. We all stood mute, unsure whether to laugh or be completely horrified.

"Iris, you have Uncle Murray all over ya!" Jax announced gleefully, breaking the uncomfortable silence. We all erupted in laughter. There was absolutely no denying it. Murray had somehow injected his humor into our ceremony, filling us with lightheartedness and joy at a time where we truly needed it.

We took the remaining ashes outside. One by one, we chose places around the yard to scatter them. The night air was unusually warm and still, and felt infused with a quiet energy. It was wonderful watching the kids as they danced around the yard, happily sprinkling the ashes of their beloved uncle in special places under the moonlight. Once we returned inside, we were amazed by the way the lights continued to flicker. Astonishingly, the fluorescent bulbs in the kitchen quit working all together about a half hour after we finished our ceremony. According to my Dad, Murray had replaced them just prior to his death.

We all remain in strong agreement that this ceremony was an extremely important step in our grieving and subsequent healing process. The timing was perfect. We were ready and very much in need of acknowledging and accepting the reality of Murray's physical death. There is no doubt that it served as an important milestone towards peace and acceptance. I think that all of us, including my father, the skeptic, would agree that Murray's energy had been present with all of us on that evening.

Chapter Twenty-Five

Third Anniversary

Being that Murray died on a national Designated Day of Remembrance, the lead up to this important yet difficult day for us was well marked. Poppies adorned our lapels several weeks beforehand and now held a mixed significance. Remembrance Day, 2008, arrived and with it a definite plan about how we were to honor and remember Murray.

The previous year we had established a ritual of a family walk through the provincial park nearby our home. Our destination was the small tree that had been planted in the memorial forest within this park in honor of Murray. For the two years past, we'd toasted Murray and the tree with a can of his favorite beer while we shivered against the November chill. On this day we had plans to do the same, and were contemplating whether or not my dad would be able to make the trek with his ailing legs.

I was just going to call my parents to solidify our plans when the phone rang. "I don't think I'll be able to make it today," my dad told me. "I woke up this morning with chest and shoulder pain and I think I should see a doctor about it. I think it might be a bit of pleurisy or then again, maybe it's just my bursitis acting up."

I told him we'd toast Murray on his behalf, and wished him luck in getting into the clinic to see a doctor swiftly. "Call us when you get home," I told him before hanging up.

The weather was unusually warm for November. As a result, the kids rode their scooters through the park as Eric and I trailed behind. When we reached Murray's tree we performed our ritual with the can of beer, sprinkling a small amount on the tree and sharing the rest. Even the kids took a tiny sip each, in honor of their beer-loving uncle. Tingles ran up and down my spine as flock after flock of geese honked loudly as they flew directly overhead. We all voiced our amazement at such timing and agreed that Murray was signifying his presence.

We arrived home rosy cheeked and refreshed from our outing. Shortly after the phone rang. It was my mom. "Dad's been taken to the hospital by ambulance," she told me breathlessly, her voice ringing with concern. "They think they found a clot in his lung and he's having trouble breathing. Could you phone emergency to find out how he's doing?" she asked.

I retrieved the phone book, looked up the hospital phone number and with trembling hands, began dialing the number for Hospital Emergency. I had a compelling, uncanny sense of déjà-vu. Three years to the day, I had made an almost identical call on behalf of my brother. Once again, I spelled out the surname "Schindelka" to the receptionist in hospital admitting, and once again, I waited with baited breath to receive news. "Please God", I breathed, don't let this be a replay of that day. Don't let my dad die on Remembrance Day too.

Relief flooded over me as the receptionist told me my dad was alive. It wasn't until we arrived at the hospital that we learned just how incredibly close my dad had come to death on that day. "Your oxygen levels were so low, we weren't sure if you'd make it or not," his doctor had informed him, while attempting to convince him just how important it was to start blood thinning treatment. My dad himself shook his head in awe over this close call. It was hard to believe that he'd almost died on the very day he'd lost his son a mere three years ago.

My dad was diagnosed as having pulmonary emboli. He was advised that to recover, he'd have to embark upon a stringent health plan that included taking blood thinners for up to a year. He was also advised to quit smoking completely. My dad had started smoking in his late teens, and had been puffing away merrily for the 50 plus years since. Apparently, if he wanted to live much longer, this would have to change.

Incredibly, with the aid of nicotine patches and an artful drawing by Iris, complete with the words, "Please stop smoking Grandpa," my dad stopped smoking cold-turkey. He has not had a cigarette since. If someone had told me prior to this that my dad would ever be capable of making this change, I would have told them they were crazy. Somehow he had found the resolve to cease a life-long habit...and had made it look easy! This experience has cause me to have a newfound level of respect and admiration for my dad. He's demonstrating an incredible amount of integrity and strength to all of us. The gift he's giving to his grandchildren is immense. Amongst other great memories of their Grandpa, they'll now remember him as a man of incredible will-power and strength.

Murray on many occasions prior to his death expressed to me his immense respect for the integrity level of my father. "He's a really good man. Better than most," Murray often told me, despite the fact that they didn't always see eye to eye. Is there significance in such a synchronicity involving the anniversary of my brother's death? I think so. Through this occurrence, my dad has been given a new lease on life. He will live out his remaining years, hopefully in a healthier state, as a non-smoker. In doing so, he's clearly demonstrating the integral man of good character that he truly is. I imagine, like all of us, Murray is very proud of his dad.

Chapter Twenty-Six

Murray's Gift to Me

When I was very young, I firmly believed that there was a place called Heaven that we went to after we died. As I grew older, my spiritual views became more focused, but I certainly had formed more questions than solid beliefs about the subject of an afterlife. I still believed that our soul lived on after death, yet I wondered about what kind of "life" we lived on the other side and what happens to our consciousness. I had never experienced solid evidence of the continuation of life after death.

Murray was well aware of my interest in the paranormal, and specifically about life after death. He often engaged me in stimulating and thought-provoking conversation. He was far more comfortable with the subject than most, bringing it up regularly, casually, and more often than not, in a humorous manner. From the talks that we had, I'm sure Murray was not at all surprised that his consciousness lived on after his body died.

Although I have always been interested in spirituality in general, I have never turned my attention to the subject of the afterlife as I have since Murray's passing. I have been rewarded beyond my wildest expectations with the abundant and mind-expanding information that Murray has conveyed to me. Along with providing certain specifics about the afterlife, my relationship with him has expanded to a new level. I get to experience the very best of what Murray is all about. I will always miss his physical presence, but to dwell on this thought, and the resultant pain that this causes, only serves to separate me from contact with him. I have learned that negative emotion such as pain and regret are not compatible with the high energies of the dimension that Murray now resides in. I now know that along with experiencing feelings of peace and joy, I must also be in a place of strong belief to clearly hear his voice. As a result, I now find myself spending much more time in this uplifted place, something that is obviously a huge benefit to my life and overall experience.

In the short time since Murray's passing, I have gained much in my lifelong spiritual quest. For that I am eternally grateful. Through my brother's death, I have received such wonderful and joyful knowledge about life. I've also realized three important truths regarding our relationships. We are eternal. There is never any separation. Love never dies.

My dear brother has shown me that every day spent in our physical bodies is a gift. It is up to each of us what we choose to do with that gift. The choices we make should be based upon whatever will bring us the highest level of joy. The achievement of joy is our indicator of success in this lifetime.

Since Murray's death I have never been more appreciative of life, love, family, and friends. Any day could be our last on this earth, so I try to enjoy every moment. These few years since Murray's passing have been the most emotional, joyful, richest years of my entire life. The gift he has bestowed upon me is monumental.

More and more I am adjusting to our new and unique relationship. It is as real and meaningful as any I have ever shared. I still receive uplifting and affirming signs and messages from Murray, but they have slowed down somewhat in their frequency and intensity, possibly because my need is not as great as it was. I now possess a constant feeling within me that Murray is not only close by, but that he is actually a part of me. I have the sense that he is a piece of the very energy of who I am. The presence of his love within me colors the way in which I see my world. The "melding" of our souls comforts me. Anytime I need Murray, he is only a thought away. I've always been a believer, but now I'm enjoying the bountiful buffet as one who "knows" the eternal nature of the soul. This "knowing" is nothing less than transformational.

Writing this book has served as a wonderful connection to Murray as well as an effective means of unearthing the many wonderful memories I have of him. As a result, it has played a huge part in my emotional healing. I have no doubt that he was instrumental in bringing me the idea of writing this book, as well as helping me to connect to the creative energies that I needed in order to do so. I have felt him throughout this process, unwaveringly by my side, gently but firmly pushing me to complete it and offering his own loving energy and input.

I believe that it is extremely important to him to share the message that life continues on after death. It's my hope that through sharing his message, I may inspire faith in others to trust that their own deceased loved ones are always close by, ready and waiting to make a connection. This faith, combined with the power of our imagination, creates the bridge from this earthly dimension to the one where our deceased loved ones reside. To simply explain away signs and messages as mere coincidences or follies of our imagination is to deny this portal to the divine. Denial creates distance between ourselves and the love that is there waiting for us. The way in which the death of our loved ones affects us, merely lies in our perspective.

I love you Murray. I could not have asked for anything more from a brother or from a friend. Thank you for all that you have given and continue to give. The door is open. I am listening. "Keep 'em comin' Cleetus!"

BOOKS

O is a symbol of the world, of oneness and unity. In different cultures it also means the "eye," symbolizing knowledge and insight. We aim to publish books that are accessible, constructive and that challenge accepted opinion, both that of academia and the "moral majority."

Our books are available in all good English language bookstores worldwide. If you don't see the book on the shelves ask the bookstore to order it for you, quoting the ISBN number and title. Alternatively you can order online (all major online retail sites carry our titles) or contact the distributor in the relevant country, listed on the copyright page.

See our website **www.o-books.net** for a full list of over 500 titles, growing by 100 a year.

And tune in to myspiritradio.com for our book review radio show, hosted by June-Elleni Laine, where you can listen to the authors discussing their books.

mySpiritRadio